By Tom McComas and James Tuohy

Lionel Collectors Series

Children's Book

Collecting Toy Trains

Video

Lionel: The Movie

Price and Rarity Guide

Lionel Postwar: 1945-1969

GREAT TOY TRAIN
LAYOUTS
of AMERICA

GREAT TOY TRAIN
LAYOUTS
of AMERICA

TOM McCOMAS and JAMES TUOHY

TM
BOOKS

Wilmette, Illinois
1987

ISBN 0-937-522-04-X
Library of Congress catalog number: 87-050508
Published by TM Books, Inc., Box 189, Wilmette, Illinois 60091
Printed in the United States of America.
First printing September, 1987

For
Nancy Adams

Contents

Acknowledgements

We originally planned to include more layouts in this book than we have. Once the production stage began we realized that more pages should be devoted to each layout than we had conceived at first. Therefore, some of the layouts that we photographed could not be used.

It was a tortuous process to decide which ones to eliminate. All of the layouts were excellent and certainly worthy of inclusion. The calls were sometimes so close as to be almost arbitrary, and we offer our apologies to those operators whose layouts do not appear here. We thank you for your cooperation and hospitality and promise if there is a sequel to this book, you will be the first to be considered.

Those who were so kind to us but who are not in this book are Ed Weidner, Graham Claytor, Tom Groff of the Choo Choo Barn, William Furnish, Karl Burkhardt, Boyd Mason, the Nassau Operating Society, Doug Ridley, Bob Board of the All Aboard Railroad, Leland Atwood of Trainland USA, the Train Collectors Museum, Dr. Greg Jones, Mel Nicholas, Don Zeiser, Doug Brooks, David Weiss, David Dansky, Barry Leonard (whose layout was built and designed by Don Cardif), Dr. Neal Schorr,

Michael Kaplan, Michael Katz, and the Toy Train Operating Society display in the California Railroad Museum.

Bob Goldsborough, a talented writer, a good friend, and an enthusiastic train fan, performed the arduous proof reading chores, assisted by Fred Schlipf of the Urbana Free Library and Dave Garrigues. Fred and Dave also provided encouragement during the project, as did Dick Christiansen of *Model Railroader* magazine, who is also editor of *Classic Toy Trains* magazine, the new Kalmbach publication.

Paul O'Toole of Unibanc Trust of Chicago believed in the project early and offered his support; he is not only a man of intuition and charm but a banker with a heart. Antoinette Algozzini has been a gracious host and patient friend through many visits and phone calls.

A special thanks is owed to the officers of the Lincoln Avenue Men with Manners Club — Michael Curley, Nelson Ghorbanian, Tom Mitoraj and Alexander Smerch.

Thanks also to Timothy Turner of Hollywood and Chicago, who is 5-feet six and a half.

Credits

All the photographs in the book were taken by Tom McComas, with the following exceptions:

Fritz von Tagen photographed Elbridge Russell's layout.

Gil and Bill Masters took the large photos of Chuck Brasher's layout.

Paul Sequeira took all the pictures of the Children's Museum and some of the pictures of Stan Roy's layout.

Ron Davis took all the photos in his chapter, plus the one we chose for the cover.

Ward Kimball submitted the large photographs used in his chapter.

Most of the views of the Lionel showroom O gauge layout first appeared in *Toy Trains* magazine, published by Carstens Publications of New Jersey. Hal Carstens graciously gave us permission to reproduce the photographs and John Van Slyke, Karl Burkhardt and Dave Garrigues were trusting enough to loan us copies of the magazine. Photographs of the Super O layout were obtained through the courtesy of Joseph Sadorf of Holland, Pennsylvania and Jim Barillaro, of Colchester, Connecticut, supplied the photos of the T-rail layout.

Michael Kolosseus and Phillip Klopp took some of the photographs used in their chapters.

Greg Dryer, a photographer and collector from Lancaster, Pennsylvania, took some of the Bruce Manson pictures.

James Campbell took the large photographs of Tom Sefton's layout.

The Alan Berliner studio of Los Angeles took the Frank Sinatra photographs.

The book was designed by Mark Finch. The dust jacket was designed by Ed Hughes, a toy train operator who recently discovered the joys of a 226E.

Introduction

Although there is much technical information in this book, we never conceived of it as primarily a nuts-and-bolts, or how-to, book. We wanted it to be a book about people and ideas and the importance of toy trains in their lives. We tell their stories and in so doing we also tell about building layouts. Not just how layouts are built, but *why* they are built.

There are essentially three types of layouts — one, a circle of track that a person puts down around the Christmas tree; two, the toy train layout with all Lionel (or American Flyer) equipment — tubular track, out-of-scale accessories, Plasticville buildings, built on a flat plywood surface sometimes covered with indoor-outdoor carpeting; and three, the hi-rail or semi-scale, a layout with real-looking T-rail track, roadbed, and ballast, as well as detailed scenery, weathered and detailed structures, ground cover and mountains and other terrain made to look like real life. Some operators vary the theme, putting an out-of-scale accessory, for example, on an otherwise scale layout.

Because the basic types of layouts are so limited, we were concerned when we started researching the project that the stories would be repetitious. Something along the lines of: "I always wanted a nice layout but didn't have the space. When I got the space I built a real nice layout and here it is. Now I'm happy running trains on this nice layout."

To a great degree, that turned out to be the general outline of the stories, but to say that simple plot line converts into repetitious stories is like saying the plot of many great plays can be summarized by saying, "Boy meets girl, boy loses girl, boy gets girl back." Or that *Moby Dick* is a story about a whale.

Every operator in this book has his own story, and each, we found, was interesting, reflecting a private concept of what he wanted his layout to represent. Each layout, while following some general outlines, is as individual as the personality of the operator who built it.

There are no track plans in the book. Originally we thought we might include them, but we changed our minds for two reasons. One, many operators didn't have track plans. Two, including track plans would mean eliminating some color photographs. Given the choice between track plans and photos, we went with photographs.

We have tried to balance two aspects of the train hobby — the human interest and an interest in technique. We trust the reader will conclude we did so — not perfectly but successfully.

An Early Layout

Some of the layouts in this book have early trains running on them. At least one, Ward Kimball's, has some trains made in the late 1800s. But those layouts were not built at the same time as the trains. In fact, all of the layouts have been built since World War II, no matter how old the trains.

We got wondering when the first layouts were built, and came to the conclusion it would be impossible to tell for sure, but one of the oldest we found was built by Elbridge Russell's dad. The layout is still in existence and how it happens to be is a pleasant tale of friendship.

Elbridge Russell was born in 1895 in Alameda, California, and lived in the same house all his life. He died there in 1984 at the age of 89. His dad first built a Carlisle & Finch layout in the attic of their two-story frame house in 1907 and that is where it stayed for the next 77 years.

The rails back in 1907 came in large, circular coils. The ties were packed separately, each with two slots through which the rails were guided. The ties were screwed to the floor, switches were added, and electricity was supplied at a full 110 volts.

For power, a circuit of five carbon filament light bulbs (inset) were wired in parallel. This circuit was wired in series with the track. The more bulbs that were turned on, lower was the resistance and more was the voltage that flowed to the track, making the trains go faster. The less lights that were on, the slower the trains went. The operator controlled the speed of the trains by screwing in or unscrewing the bulbs.

Russell and his dad eventually built three layouts in their attic. In addition to the Carlisle & Finch, they built a Lionel O gauge with 32

1

Carlisle & Finch's first locomotive, the mining engine. The very earliest of these were made in 1897-98 and used a rubber band belt drive, but clockwork-style gears were used beginning in 1899. The type in the picture was introduced about 1906.

Voltamp made some Pacific Fruit Express cars especially for the Pan American Expo in San Francisco in 1915. The one behind the mining engine and coal cars is the only one known to have stripes under the roofwalk.

switches and a No. 1 layout featuring Voltamp Interurbans. All three layouts were screwed directly to the floor, and all remained there until 1984.

A few years before he died, Russell became friends with Fritz von Tagen, a toy train enthusiast and the photographer who did the 1987 Lionel catalog. One day they visited Russell's attic, where he hadn't been since 1950.

"Everything was covered with dust," said von Tagen, "but you could clearly make out the three layouts, trains still on the tracks, just as they were left thirty years ago."

Von Tagen and Russell eventually got the trains running again.

"I started first on the O gauge layout. I took up all 32 switches, cleaned and oiled them, and then replaced the old wires with new. We cleaned and oiled all the engines and the rolling stock.

"You could see Elbridge brighten as we got more trains to run. I cleaned and oiled the Carlisle & Finch trains and got them working. The easiest of all was the Voltamp. Those trolleys were the smoothest and best running trains I have ever seen."

Someone who agrees with that evaluation is Graham Claytor, the president of Amtrak and a collector of old trains. In 1984 Claytor restored some old Carlisle & Finch himself and made a layout for Christmas.

"Most things — and people — who are 70 to 85 years old don't run quite as well as they used to," said Claytor in a article he wrote about building his floor layout. "But that generalization doesn't apply to these great trains. Every one I have found can, with only minor cleaning or repair, be made to operate

Another view of Elbridge Russell's layout. Built by his father in 1907, structures were added to it over the years, such as the landscaped diner in the '30s and the floodlight and signal tower back in the '20s.

almost as well as the day it came from the store."

Once von Tagen and Russell cleaned up the trains and the layout they began to play with them frequently.

"Elbridge used to run seven trains at once over the three layouts. He would be jumping back and forth between the controls, screwing and unscrewing light bulbs on the Carlisle & Finch layout, switching switches on the Lionel layout and adjusting the transformers on the Voltamp layout. He was really good."

Russell's eyesight was poor and he needed help to see the switches, so von Tagen went to a train meet and bought a bunch of Lionel billboards. These he converted into cards with large numbers and placed them next to the switches

on the layout. He put corresponding numbers on the switch levers on the control panel.

"He was delighted," said von Tagen. "There were two happy guys up in that attic playing with toy trains."

Eventually von Tagen moved to Portland, Oregon, but he still flew down to Alameda every few months to "play trains with Elbridge."

Then in 1984 Russell died. A short time later his widow, Carol, told von Tagen that Russell wanted him to have the trains. Von Tagen disassembled the Voltamp and Lionel layouts, but he wanted to keep the Carlisle & Finch intact, which was not easy.

"I unscrewed the ties and lifted the whole thing up on bamboo poles,"

he said. "Then I slid four-by-eight sections of plywood underneath and disconnected the track only over the breaks in the plywood. I never even took the screws out of the ties."

He put everything back together once back in his Portland home, where the photographs of the layout used in this book were taken.

Fritz von Tagen is 40 years old, a half century younger than Eldridge Russell. But von Tagen said he considered Russell his best friend.

"He was the nicest man I ever met," said von Tagen, who has been offered quite a bit of money to sell Russell's trains. "I was glad to get the trains because I would have something to remember Elbridge. There is no way I will ever sell any of this stuff."

Chuck Brasher
Grass Valley, California

Chuck, Suzie and Eileen Brasher

A Suitable Environment for Standard Gauge Classics

Tucked under a stand of Ponderosa pines among the foothills of the Sierra Nevada mountains, the Colonial house of Chuck Brasher was designed to accommodate several important requirements.

Brasher, a contractor, wanted the house to be an authentic replica of the first homes built in New England in the 18th Century, right down to the wood planking and square nails; he did not want any trees on the homestead to be destroyed; and integrated into the design would be a room suitable for a vast standard gauge layout.

Brasher succeeded in meeting all the goals he set for himself. The gabled and clapboard home, nestled halfway between Sacramento and Lake Tahoe, is rustically accurate and surrounded by unviolated trees; and Chuck Brasher has one of the finest standard gauge layouts in the country.

"When we decided to move to Northern California, I designed the house with this layout room in mind," said Brasher, 48, who was born in the Los Angeles area and married his wife, Suzie, there in 1963. "I wanted the train room to have no doors, few windows, and the entrance stairway in the middle. I don't like to have to duck under or raise a bridge to get into the center of the layout."

To achieve what he wanted, Brasher selected a second floor area for the train room. It is directly above the front entrance. A stairway from the front hall leads to the middle of his table top layout, which reaches 40 feet at its longest stretch, then doglegs to the left, as the golfers say, for another 20 feet at one end. The layout is 20 feet wide throughout, with seven of those feet left open in the middle for operating and viewing space. It is in this viewing space that the stairwell sits, at the dogleg end. Trains from Brasher's collection sit on shelves at both ends of the room, ready to be run as the mood strikes him.

(continued on page 8)

5

Uncommon rarity is a common virtue on Chuck Brasher's layout. ABOVE The Blue Comet and State sets pass in front of the 128 city station and terrace. Brasher intentionally kept the color of the table top a neutral brown in order not to compete with the bright colors of the trains and accessories. LEFT A night scene featuring Ives Black Diamond passenger cars.

OPPOSITE TOP The seldom seen orange roof version of Lionel's 437 switch tower and the rare, late version of the Hell Gate bridge bracket the American Flyer Pocahontas set. That's a nickel-trimmed 385 pulling Ives transition cars across the bridge. OPPOSITE LOWER LEFT Four 444 roundhouse sections, one of the most sought after Lionel accessories. OPPOSITE LOWER RIGHT The Flyer 4695 with nickel trim is rare. Most were made with brass trim.

Brasher operates American Flyer, Ives, Dorfan and Lionel. He has every good standard gauge train ever made, including the State Set, Blue Comet, President's Special, and the Ives Olympian. He also has about every good accessory there is, including four Lionel roundhouse sections and the Dorfan crane.

"I love accessories. There are only a few color variations that I don't have. At least there are only a few color variations I'm looking for. When I started collecting, everyone put their trains on shelves. Nobody ran trains. That's why accessories weren't in demand. I started going after accessories from the beginning."

Although Brasher's father set up an American Flyer O gauge train every year at Christmas time, Chuck didn't become really interested in the train hobby until he was 28 years old and married for two years. He had kept the old Flyer O gauge train through the years, and one day Suzie discovered it packed away and decided to get it fixed in running condition. They took it to Ron Wade, a collector who was to become a good friend.

"I remember walking into Ron's garage. There were all kinds of trains and parts and track. I was amazed. Ron took us into his train room, where he had stuff on shelves on the walls. He had O gauge and standard gauge. I had never seen standard gauge before and I was hooked."

That was 1966. Brasher joined the Toy Train Operating Society, a collector's club headquartered on the West Coast, and began an earnest hunt for trains.

"I decided to concentrate on standard gauge, so I would sell off all the O and S gauge to buy standard."

Brasher, however, never restricted himself to accumulating trains. He wanted to operate them.

Accessories abound in Grass Valley, including some of the best of Ives and Dorfan. CLOCKWISE FROM TOP LEFT The Ives 123 double station, a collecting masterpiece, was cataloged from the early 1900s through the early 1920s, with the early versions having colored glass panels and the later versions clear glass. . . . The hybrid Ives crossing gate — with the 3245 Olympian passing by — cataloged from 1928 through 1930, has an Ives base and fence, American Flyer shed and Lionel barrier (this version is illuminated and has brass window inserts, an even rarer model has no light and a rubber stamped window frame). . . . The lithographed Ives freight station was made in 1917 only and is a real rarity. . . . The coveted Dorfan crane, made in 1930 only, is, except for the tin cab, entirely die cast, with gears that work well but have a tendency to decay. . . . An original Ives water tower.

In the train yard, from the top: the Lionel 400E freight set, the Blue Comet, American Flyer 1929 President's Special, Ives Black Diamond, Lionel 9 set in orange, the Dorfan uncataloged 3932.

"When I started, it was rare to find an operating layout in all of the Los Angeles area. It was almost that if you asked if the train ran then you weren't a collector. I ran trains from the beginning. Even when we lived in an apartment. I nailed the track right to the floor and ran the trains. I couldn't wait until we had the space for my layout."

Brasher spent three weeks working on the plans for his Grass Valley layout. He said he doubts that the finished layout deviated by more than 5 per cent from his original drawings.

An Ives lightbulb box sits on a 161 Lionel baggage truck, which is on a 155 Lionel freight station.

There are only two flat wall surfaces in Brasher's angular train room. He uses those surfaces to display his collection.

The Dorfan 3932 engine headed the Black Diamond Express (not to be confused with the Ives Black Diamond cars shown on page 6). The set number, 901, was put on the engine, which was highly unusual. It was made in 1927 only.

Both Lionel and American Flyer made standard gauge switch towers in two sets of color combinations. ABOVE The two versions of the 108 American Flyer switch tower are eagerly sought after by collectors, but the version on the left is easier to find than the version on the right. BELOW The 437 Lionel switch tower on the left is much easier to find than the rare, orange-roofed version on the right.

"I took each accessory I was going to use on the layout and measured it, the height, the width. Then I started designing a track plan that would accommodate all the accessories and still get the most switches and the most crossings and the most track in the space I had.

"I wanted to make a layout that used the trains the way they were intended to be used. Freight trains with freight accessories and passenger trains with passenger accessories. I wanted to make it as good as I could for a table top layout without getting into the ballast and the mountains those scale guys do.

"Size and color had a lot to do with where I placed stuff on the layout. I like the Ives glass-domed station, the Flyer Union station, the Lionel 921 landscape with nine houses, the roundhouses."

Color also played an important part in the selection of the material Brasher used for deadening the sound and the type of lights he employed.

"I like the brown color of the sound board. It's neutral. The trains have so much color I didn't want the surface of the table to compete in any way. I didn't want green indoor-outdoor carpet, for instance. With the lights, incandescent fixtures are built into the beams. I didn't want fluorescent lighting because it alters the colors of the trains. I thought of track lighting on the ceiling, but that's too modern. It's not in keeping with the period of my house."

There are 550 feet of standard gauge track on Brasher's layout. There are three different loops and 17 sidings. All that in operation causes quite a racket unless insulated.

"I used one-half-inch sound deadening board on top of the plywood table top. Next, my daughter,

(continued on page 16)

This Lionel scenic park came in three sections, two curved ends and a middle. It is hard to find complete. Usually the middle section is missing. Brasher has all three on his layout, a collector's delight.

The nerve center of Chuck Brasher's layout. The middle of the three control panels, to the left of the transformer, has a silver base, the rarest of all Lionel control panels.

The bridges are American Flyer, the sets Lionel — the number 54
with the 18, 19 and 190 cars and the Blue Comet.

The Lionel Hell Gate bridge in the late colors of silver, ivory and red.
Before 1935 Lionel painted most of its structures in combinations of
green, cream and terra cotta. The earlier Hell Gate had cream
portals, green span and terra cotta base.

The American Flyer Union Station was impressive but flimsy. Very few have survived. Available in 1928 only, it was made of silk-screened cardboard and rested on a landscaped, half-inch pine base. It came with five lights and two brass eagles. This one is in like-new condition and is priceless.

The later version of the Lionel 128 terrace station. This had the 115 station house. The earlier one had the 124 station.

Eileen, cut thousands of foam rubber strips and we inserted them under each tie so only the foam touches the table surface. I didn't use many screws to secure the track, about one every three feet. Then I put a rubber grommet between each screw and tie. So the track sort of floats on the rubber grommet and the foam rubber.

"I would like to have Lionel's rubber roadbed, but there just isn't enough around. It took Tom Sefton 20 years to get enough for his layout."

Both daughter Eileen and wife Suzie helped Brasher construct the layout. Eileen soldered the wire connections, scooting about on a creeper. After the layout was built Eileen went to Japan as a high school exchange student. She helped finance the trip by selling five Lionel Disney handcars her father had given her when she was a child. Suzie returned to college in her mid-forties to get a nursing degree.

One side of the layout contains a passenger yard with a station, the

other side the freight yard and roundhouse area. An elevated section goes completely around the layout so that all the bridges, except one at table level, are functional. There are display shelves on either end of the layout, and the rest of the collection is kept in boxes beneath.

Brasher is partial to freight cars. "I have every color variation of the 200 series freight cars, including the early ones and the nickel trim ones. I have all the color variations of Flyer and Ives I can find. For looks I like Ives. I have a full set of the Flyer-Ives transition cars. Then I have the Lionel-Ives tank car, gondola, crane and caboose. Ives made lots of different colors of the same car, and I like to find one I don't have. As for accessories, the hardest to find are the Ives transition and Dorfan trackside accessories."

Brasher said the best of all his engines are American Flyer.

"They're my best runners, the smoothest and quietest. I have some good Lionel runners, the 408s in particular, but the Flyer motors are the best."

This is the first permanent layout Brasher has ever made. He feels he might have done some things better. He would like more and longer sidings, for instance. "You want to minimize putting the trains on the track and taking them off by hand,

which sidings allow one to avoid." And he said he would like more grades and water scenes to break up the flat surface of the table.

But all in all, Chuck Brasher's layout is an outstanding accomplishment, a working environment for some of the most valuable items in train collecting.

"I'm proud," he said. "Satisfied. How could I not be?"

The end of the line. Four sections of the largest accessory Lionel ever made - the 444 roundhouse.

Children's Museum
Indianapolis, Indiana

A Rememberance of Things Past

The Children's Museum of Indianapolis occupies 203,000 square feet on five levels of a modern building at 30th and Meridian, making it the largest museum of its kind in the world. It is devoted strictly to kids.

The O gauge layout there is 32x32 feet and is located on the top floor in its own gallery section, along with a smaller room containing an HO layout and one holding the largest public display of old toy trains in the world. The 5,000-piece display is composed of what used to be the private collections of two Indiana businessmen.

The entire exhibit is called Toy Train Treasuries and is on the same floor as a full-size carousel and a couple of miniature doll houses. On the floor below, among other things, is an old log cabin and on the ground level is a Victorian train station and an 0-10-0 woodburning loco named the Reuben Wells, which went into service in Madison, Indiana, in 1868 and was a sort of engineering marvel because its regular route was up a 5.89 per cent grade called Madison Hill.

The toy trains on the fifth floor of the Children's Museum came from the collections of two late tinplaters, Robert Vickers of Anderson,

OPPOSITE The layout as it looked when it opened in 1976. An airport has since replaced the western town. The layout is operated from the control tower. ABOVE The grain elevator was scratch-built, but the layout also contains Plasticville houses and Lionel stations.

The mountains were formed with wood fiber plaster over a screen wire base supported by 1x2s. The layout is designed so a person can walk on it for maintenance and repair chores.

and Noble Biddinger of Indianapolis. The collection is exhibited in eight-foot high glass cases with special lighting that allows one to examine items closely without casting a shadow on the glass. It includes American Flyer, American Miniature, Beggs, Boucher, Buddy "L," Carlisle & Finch, Dayton-Dinky, Dorfan, Electoy, General, Howard, Ives, Knapp, Lionel and Voltamp, in addition to foreign makers like Marklin, Bing, Karl Bub, Carette and Hornby.

The collection, as well as an earlier layout that measured 18x24, used to be in another building. Although the Children's Museum was established in 1925, it has had several

locations and, the present building was not opened until October of 1976. In March of 1976 work was started on the current layout.

The layout was built by Les and Helen Gordon, owners of Gordon's Hobbies of Indianapolis, who worked on the project, along with their son, George, and three helpers, for five months.

"Since it was for a museum, we wanted to show how a toy train layout could depict life in America," said Helen Gordon. "We wanted to create scenes that trains really go by. We wanted to be realistic, but we still wanted it to look like a toy train layout."

The Gordons also wanted to illustrate some different ways trains were used, since the kids who visit the museum don't know. They've grown up in an age of air transportation, as well as trucking on super highways.

"Trains went by farms, so we built farms," said Helen Gordon. "Circuses traveled by rail, so we have a circus. Passenger stations and freight yards, too."

The layout has a scale-modeler look to it. Campbell kits were used for some buildings, but others are scratch built, as is one of the most impressive structures on the layout,

(continued on page 25)

The trains on the layout are exclusively MPC, although when it opened they were postwar Lionel. ABOVE The long, graceful arch bridge was scratch-built by the Gordons. An Erie Lackawanna GP-20 passes in front of the airport that replaced the raucous old western town. RIGHT The roundhouse was built from a scale kit put out by Placer Nevada and El Dorado RR of Roseville, California, a company now out of business. When the layout was expanded and a bigger roundhouse was needed, Les Gordon scratch-built three more stalls.

The mountains at the Children's Museum are as realistic as those on any layout in the country. They have access holes inside them.

OPPOSITE TOP The circus tents and wagons were made from kits — the tents from Modern Hobbies of Utica, New York, and the wagons from Wardie Jay. OPPOSITE BOTTOM The trees providing shade near the Lionel station were made from dried baby's breath. Other trees on the layout were made from either baby's breath or Truscale kits.

ABOVE Three different levels provide visual borders that separate residential, business, and rural areas. LEFT The bustling freight yards are passed over by a truss bridge. The track is Gargraves. OPPOSITE The farm lies in a meadow below the airport and spreads under the elegant arch bridge.

an arch bridge that runs gracefully along much of one side. It competes for attention with a ten-stall roundhouse. And looming over everything — the switch yard, farms, towns, and the bustling circus — are mountains as realistically detailed as one will find on any layout in the country.

The Gordons designed a track plan that includes five independent loops that operate on three different levels. The 900 feet of track is Gargraves. Most of the equipment that operates now is MPC, although the Gordons put on postwar Lionel when the new museum building opened.

The layout is enclosed on three sides by glass partitions. The fourth side is a wall and on it is the control panel, housed in a tower that is built to look like a switchman's watch tower.

George Gordon is an electrical engineer and he installed some stunning illumination. The ceiling is painted flat black to eliminate reflection. The non-glare surface allows subtle lighting changes from spotlights that rain down from the ceiling. There is less light in the non-populated areas, like mountains, and more light in the towns.

The Children's Museum layout even has had it own urban renewal program. There is an airport that the Gordons did not build.

"Originally we had an old time western town, with saloons and gambling halls, but they tore it down and put in the airport," said Helen Gordon. "I guess they elected a reform mayor who wanted to rid the town of vice."

Ron Davis and Bill Taylor
Cleveland, Ohio

Ron Davis and Bill Taylor

Scale Accuracy in an O Gauge Setting

Ron Davis received his first Lionel, the Seaboard work train set, as a Christmas present in 1954, when he was 6 years old. As is not uncommon among train collectors, that first offer of affection led to a lifelong love affair that seems to intensify rather than diminish.

Twenty-five years later, when Davis and his first cousin, Bill Taylor, decided to build a layout, a decision had to be made that would test Davis's love of Lionel.

"I had built layouts every year from the time I was seven until I was 16," said Davis, who is now 38 and a manufacturer of trophies. "I had accessories on all the layouts I built, but Bill and I both wanted everything to be in scale and as realistic as possible. That meant no Lionel accessories. We wanted an O-scale layout. I even considered O-scale trains — not Lionel — but I love Lionel. I've collected for over 30 years. Lionel is part of my life."

Davis decided to use Lionel trains but keep everything else in scale. For instance, the buildings are recognizable as Lionel and Plasticville, but only by their shapes. Taylor, a skilled modeler who did all the scenic work, constructed the buildings out of building kits. He painted, weathered and detailed each one to give it scratch-built realism.

Ron Davis likes to run F-3s, his favorite engine; he has the entire series. Shown above are the Burlington, Rio Grande, and Western Pacific. His favorites are the Canadian Pacific and B&O.

Although predominantly Lionel, the motive power is not exclusively so. This is a Williams model of the New York Central's streamlined Hudson, with the distinctive Roman sentinel snout (Lionel's model of the unstreamlined Hudson is also shown). The pilot trucks of the Williams model kept bouncing off the track, so Davis added a spring to hold them on better. "William's stuff looks good but you always have to make some adjustments to make it run properly," says Davis.

Two kits were combined to create this oversized Rico Station.

"If you make the buildings and leave them the way they come, they have a toy-plastic look," said Taylor one Friday evening as he watched his cousin ease forward on the throttles of a Lionel ZW transformer. A 2383 Canadian Pacific F-3 picked up speed as it swung out of a curve.

"For example, that small Lionel station: I painted and weathered the sides to make them look like real wood, and the chimney, like real brick. Then I added windows and fixtures and other detailing. The whole thing comes to life. It's a touch. An eye. Either you have it or you don't."

Davis and Taylor built the layout during six months of 1979. Their attention to scenic detail has resulted in a layout that in some ways has more impact than a full-scale HO spread. The trains are so much bigger. The layout is

sprinkled with tools, barrels, sacks and other paraphernalia, as well as men carrying some of these things near the trains, while stylistically correct autos and trucks hover nearby. All this is in accurate proportion to the trains, and the hulking presence of a 773 Hudson next to a worker throwing sacks on a baggage cart offers a real-life feeling of the contrast between man and the gigantic machines he is capable of creating. The sheer size of an O gauge engine has the ability, when placed next to scale workmen and equipment, to produce a more intense verisimilitude than the smaller gauges, no matter how much more accurate detail these might afford.

While Taylor, 42, a professional photographer who specializes in pictures of real trains, did the modeling, Davis did the wiring and track. The one-level layout is located in the basement of their

aunt's home. It is wedge-shaped, measuring 18 feet at the wide end, 20 feet on the sides and 12 feet at the narrow end. The controls are in a cut-out area in the center. There are three independent loops and numerous sidings.

"My main thought was to get as much of my collection as possible on the track. I wasn't concerned about switching from one loop to another," said Davis. "I'm a collector but mainly an operator. I have an almost complete postwar collection in excellent-plus condition, but I run everything I have. That's what the trains were made to do."

Although Davis has placed his entire Lionel collection on the tracks at one time or another, he has not kept the layout an exclusively Lionel operation. He has thrown in a few other things. Rolling stock includes Weaver

29

PF-2 hoppers and two and three-bay hoppers, and an Atlas caboose which has been kitbashed and customized. Much of the O gauge Lionel rolling stock has also been repainted and customized. Motive power is from both postwar eras of Lionel and from Williams.

"The engines from 1956 and 1957, like the Canadian Pacific and Baltimore & Ohio, seem to run best," said Davis. "I never intended to buy as much MPC as I have, but they have made such nice stuff, like the SD-40, I can't resist.

"I've had problems operating my Daylight. It starts out strong, pulling nine of the aluminum passenger cars, but after awhile I have to keep upping the throttle. With the older engines, I can pull 13 or 14 of the passenger cars for hours, no problem. I think it's something MPC does differently with the armature, but I don't know what."

Power is supplied by the ZW transformer for the mainline and a Troller Solid State transformer for the other two lines. The trains run on Lionel Super O track.

The scale track signals were purchased from NJ Custom Brass. They are activated by a light sensor system designed by Fricko Hobbies of Cincinnati.

Davis and Taylor operate the trains every Friday night. "We try to be historically and geographically accurate," said Taylor. "We try to run trains from the same era and part of the country. For example, we'll run the Hudson with GG-1s and NYC F-3s. Or if someone comes over who is a Santa Fe nut, we'll run Santa Fes and other Western roads."

A log is kept each time an engine is run, and it is lubricated every third time on the track. Davis said the key to minimizing troubles is

Davis and Taylor have created a quality of scale detailing seldom seen on a toy train layout. OPPOSITE TOP The cars and trucks are Revell kits and repainted Matchbox. OPPOSITE BOTTOM Taylor weathered and detailed a Heljan O scale engine house and replaced the European-style smokestack with an American style. The figures are both plastic and metal, hand-painted. ABOVE The 8376 Union Pacific SD-40. For routine maintenance Labelle 107 lightweight oil is used on the axles, side rods and gears. Each engine gets an annual overhaul, which includes replacing the brushes and cleaning the armature and commutator. The track is cleaned with green 3M scouring pads.

The layout uses Super O track throughout. It looks good, and Davis and Taylor had a lot of it to start with. Although the first switches they used were Super O, they later switched to Gargraves. "Super O switches just don't work very well, and you can't get parts for them," says Davis. Davis and Taylor are not timid about operating valuable collector pieces. "If it's got a motor in it, we run it," says Taylor. BELOW Two Lackwanna FMs. RIGHT Lionel grain elevator weathered and detailed by Bill Taylor.

to build good benchwork and have level track. If he had it to do over again, Davis said he would be a little neater with the wiring.

"I've got spaghetti under there. I also wish I had used something over the plywood, like Homosote, to deaden the sound."

But those are minor concerns. Both Ron Davis and Bob Taylor said they feel satisfied they have accomplished what they set out to do. Improvements can be made later.

"A layout is never done," said Taylor. "You can add fine detail forever."

Bill Taylor, a professional photographer of real trains, creates the lonesome mood of trains passing through a small town at night.

Ralph Johnson
Los Angeles, California

Bob Ziegler, Nick Barone, Ralph Johnson, Steve Marinkovich

34

A Firm Foundation in Friendship

A labor of love.

That is what the building of Ralph Johnson's layout was.

After his original layout was destroyed, Ralph Johnson's friends, some working hundreds of hours, helped him build another one.

Johnson is old, his friends are young. Johnson is black, his friends are white. It does not matter. Love does not care about those things.

Johnson, 75, worked for years for, among others, the Southern Pacific Railroad and H & M Steamship Lines. He is a past president and director emeritus of the Southwest Division of the Toy Train Operating Society.

"I bought my first Lionel train when I was 18," he said, standing near the garage he enlarged years ago to accommodate his layout. "I had an apartment in Oakland and used to run the train on the wood floor late at night. This old Japanese lady lived downstairs and used to pound on my door to get me to stop making so much noise.

"I loved Lionel trains all my life. I kept looking forward to retirement because then I knew I'd have all the time I needed to operate the trains."

After he retired Johnson got what he wanted. He enlarged his garage to accommodate as fine a layout as existed in the Los Angeles area. He was president of the TTOS, surrounded by friends who shared his great passion for trains.

ABOVE   Scale structures dot the landscape. Steve Marinkovich spent 130 hours building this switch tower. Everything, inside and out, was scratch-built, including the window frames, staircase, and interior light fixture, which was formed from a flat piece of brass. The chimney was made from a solid piece of balsa, with bricks scribed in and chipped to represent aging.

OPPOSITE   Ralph Johnson's 37x17-foot layout has two mainlines and is dominated by beautifully crafted mountains. Johnson used 20 colors to capture the subtle changes of real mountains.

The mountainside contains a lake and waterfall whose realism was achieved by over 100 hours of labor. Barone painted the plaster black where the water was to appear deep, then detailed it in shades of brown and brushed on acrylic gloss medium. The rapids effect under the bridge and at the bottom of the falls was accomplished by pressing unraveled cotton balls into the acrylic while it was still wet, then coating them with aqua blue oil paint, highlighted with white.

Then things started to go badly for Ralph Johnson. His wife became incurably ill from cancer. While attending to her during her long sickness, he neglected the layout in the garage.

"He had been caring for Dorothy and didn't have time for anything else," said Nick Barone, a friend and fellow TTOS officer. Barone, at 30, is 45 years younger than Johnson but they have known each other since Barone was 18.

"Ralph was down and I thought it would help to get the trains running again."

What had once been a mighty train layout was now a rather disreputable hulk. Water, coming from a leak in the ceiling, had destroyed the scenery, and the creosote roadbed was crumbling. Rats had eaten away the wiring.

"I felt bad because I know Ralph really loves his trains," said Barone. "He taught me everything about trains. He has a super-big heart. He's like a dad to me. I love the guy."

Barone called Bob Ziegler, another TTOS member and a wiring expert

who designs security systems for banks.

"I knew it was going to be a lot of work and I wouldn't have considered doing it for anybody else but Ralph Johnson," said Ziegler, who is 32.

Ziegler first attempted to repair the existing wiring while Barone, a mechanical engineer, tried to repair the scenery. They soon decided it would be better to start anew, which they did in May of 1985. By November the new wiring was installed and the trains were running again, but everything else was chaotically under construction. The

20-by-40-foot room was filled with piles of plaster and a variety of rubbish. Besides the gridwork, wiring and track, only a large freight yard in the center gave a suggestion of the grandeur that once was.

Then just after Thanksgiving, Dorothy Johnson died.

Nick Barone and Bob Ziegler went to the memorial services. They were concerned about Johnson.

"Ralph was sort of lost," said Ziegler. "He needed something to get involved in. To occupy his mind."

At about the same time, the authors of this book were compiling information about the best layouts across the country. They had heard about Ralph Johnson's splendid layout in Los Angeles and had sent a letter asking if they could photograph it the following February. They did not know it was currently under reconstruction. The letter arrived at Ralph Johnson's house the day after his wife's funeral.

Barone, Ziegler and Johnson talked things over and decided to have a layout worthy of inclusion in the book ready by February. So what if the shooting date was only 10 weeks away? So what if Nick Barone and Bob Ziegler had full-time and demanding jobs? It would be good for Ralph.

"The letter couldn't have come at a better time," said Barone. "The idea of being in that book lifted his spirits. You could see the change."

More help was needed. Barone enlisted his friend, Steve Marinkovich, a 29-year-old longshoreman and a skilled scenery maker. It was decided to make the layout as realistic as possible, using scratch-built or scale-detailed accessories. They would use Lionel 072 switches,

The layout has the look of the Southwest, and Johnson runs trains with road names associated with the area. The freight yards can hold 110 cars, which are guided by 20 Lionel 072 switches and two 022 switches.

On the mainline above the turntable: Kusan passenger cars, custom-painted in the colors of the Southern Pacific, Johnson's favorite roadname.

"We are especially proud of our track work," says Barone, who said they used gray, light brown and dark brown Woodland Scenics ballast, which was placed around the ties with a plastic spoon. To keep the ballast in place, they sprayed on a 4 to 1 mixture of water and white glue, which dries clear but doesn't look wet.

which are dependable, and some plastic buildings — but not without detailing them.

The mountains were built first. Johnson mixed over 20 colors to duplicate the subtle changes in color of real mountains. He has an unorthodox method of application.

"I do it with a straw," he said. "First, I moisten the surface with water out of a spray bottle. Then I hold the mixture of powdered dye and plaster in my hands and blow it onto the mountain through a straw. Then I spray water on again and the dry dye and plaster bind together. In some arid areas I use shades of brown, other areas, like near the waterfall, are more green. Comes out looking dry and like a real mountain."

The high standards the team set for itself began to take a toll. It took more than 100 hours to build the lake and waterfall on the mountainside. The ballast is very realistic and was extremely time consuming to construct. To do 15 feet of double mainline took two men three hours. There are 1,000 feet of track on the layout.

In early December Mark Depew, a 30-year-old banker and member of an HO modeling club, joined the team. He built stone walls and helped Steve Marinkovich build the city. The number of days and nights and hours each man worked began to increase. The project started with two men working two nights a week. In December four men were working four nights a week. In January they began work-

ing five nights a week and every weekend.

By February there were five men on the project — Johnson, Barone, Ziegler, Marinkovich and Depew. The night before the scheduled shooting they were all there, all working, as they had been so many nights before.

"The five of us worked all night," said Ziegler. "We slept in shifts. By morning we were all dirty, tired and soaking wet from a new leak on the roof, but the layout was finished and the leak was fixed."

It is a marvelous layout — clean of line and as open as the mountainous Southwest. There are dogs and cows about the yards and waysides, and one almost expects to see a

People and animals are sprinkled throughout the layout, caught in realistic stop-action.

The two mainlines are independent loops. Each has a siding capable of holding 15 freight cars and four engines, or a seven-foot passenger train. Power is supplied by four Lionel ZW transformers — one each for the mainlines, one for the yard, and one for the lights, relays, and switches.

sun-bleached steer skull. The trains are mostly Lionel, from both the postwar and MPC eras, but just about every manufacturer is represented, including Kris, Williams, Kusan, KMT, and even some scale, scratch-built rolling stock outfitted with Lionel trucks and couplers. The road names are Western, Johnson's favorites; Santa Fe, Southern Pacific and Union Pacific predominate.

"I'm proud of all this," said Nick Barone, his arm sweeping the rail-road panorama. "We wanted to do these things on our own layouts but we sacrificed that because Ralph is such a good friend. We love him."

Everyone gained by the experience, said Marinkovich.

"It was like a team going through a season. At first you don't know each other so well. You spend a lot of time together, overcome adversities, and by the time it's over, you have established friendships that will last a lifetime."

Bob Ziegler, standing nearby, looked at the layout and then at Ralph Johnson.

"We wanted to make a realistic layout," he said. "But we wanted to make Ralph happy, too. I think we accomplished both goals. Seeing the smile on Ralph's face when the layout was finished and the trains were running again was enough payment for all of us."

The dictionary does not define it better.

A labor of love.

"We wanted a scale modeler's layout that operated Lionel trains," says Barone. "We would make a few concessions, like having some Lionel plastic buildings, but they would have to be detailed and weathered."

The Lionel engines have been modified, replacing E units with electronic ATRU units from GSI and replacing nylon gears with brass gears. The ATRU units operate on a time delay so engines won't drop into neutral accidently.

A Southern Pacific Daylight sweeps into a graceful
curve. Gargraves track was shaped into 12-foot
diameter curves because Johnson has a number of
scale kit cars that could not negotiate an 072 curve.

Ward Kimball
San Gabriel, California

Amid the Orange Trees, a History Lesson

Ward Kimball, standing next to a five-loop layout, watched through black, goggle-rimmed eyeglasses as the trolley clacked over crude metal rails on wood crossties. It was a Lionel number 300 trolley, with "City Hall Park" written on it.

"I've never seen it run anywhere else," said Kimball, referring to Lionel's early 2⅞-inch gauge, which dates to 1902. The handful of 2⅞-inch gauge items that were made were sold store-to-store by Joshua Lionel Cowen himself, the very first trains he made.

"I've never even *seen* it anywhere else," said a fascinated visitor.

There is much on Ward Kimball's layout that most people have never seen, and certainly have never seen run, anywhere else.

Kimball's layout — his whole collection, actually, which includes two layouts in two different rooms of a structure he calls his "train building" — is not so much a display as a history lesson.

"There are no doubt larger collections but this probably has the most rarity in terms of age," said Kimball. "I have collected the whole history of toy train manufacture from 1870 to 1940."

Indeed, when Kimball first began collecting in 1946, he was attracted by the esthetics of an item and how it was made, rather than its rarity or value as a collector's piece.

"I didn't know how much they were worth," said Kimball. "I would buy old trains — they were called antiques then — because I liked them and wanted to keep a historical record. Burton Logan, who started the Train Collectors Association, would visit us often and help us identify the old stuff I had. He'd say: 'That's a Howard. That's a rare train.' I didn't know one manufacturer from another."

Gradually, though, Kimball learned. He became a charter member of the Train Collectors Association when it was formed in 1954 and eventually its president.

He hunted trains wherever he could and had one valuable contact not far from San Gabriel, which is just south of Pasadena.

"I knew a woman who appraised old estates in Pasadena. When they would break up these estates she would call me if there were any trains or toys."

Now Kimball's exceptional collection is housed in a 60-foot-long building in his backyard. One room contains his collection of American trains and the other his European models.

The layouts are not elaborate. If it were not for what is on them, and perhaps the large space he has, the layouts would be no different from hundreds of others around the country. There are two layout tables. One measures 12x14 feet, the other 10x18 feet, both 42 inches high, without scenery or fancy ballasting. The tables are screwed together. There are no nails. They can be disassembled and carried out the door. He has

Ward Kimball has two layout rooms — The American Room, above, representing U.S. manufacturers, and the European Room, page 42, with foreign makers.

Lionel 2⅞-inch trolley operating on the first track Lionel made.

five loops of varying gauges in the American room and four loops in the European room. Each loop is controlled by a separate transformer.

"My overriding concern was running the trains," said Kimball. "I wanted to watch them *go*. That's the fun of it for me. I didn't want anything fancy. I didn't want to have any derailments."

The very thought of Kimball running some of the trains he does would cause most collectors to hyperventilate. If they had what he has they would probably keep them behind vacuum-sealed glass. As he stood watching the Converse-bodied 2⅞-inch trolley clatter around its loop, he could glance at the other loops and see a Lionel number 10 interurban or an American Flyer Statesman set in standard gauge, a Voltamp 2100 electric in 2-inch gauge, or the Ives 1129 and 3240 electrics in number 1 gauge. And that was only a quick glance.

On shelves on the walls of the American room is the complete history of toy trains. One wall is devoted to early tin, wood and cast iron trackless floor trains: Ives, Althof-Bergmann, Welker-Crosby, Crandall, George Brown, Reed, Bliss, Milton Bradley — all identified with labels, containing names and dates of manufacture, on the edge of the shelves.

A section of one wall contains the definitive cast iron collection, including Secor Carpenter, Pratt & Letchworth, Kenton, Ives, Ideal, Hubley, Harris, Stevens, and Wilkins. Early electrics are in another section: Carlisle & Finch, Knapp, Howard, Voltamp, and Elektoy, along with the complete line of Lionel 2⅞-inch.

One of Kimball's favorite displays is Ives. He has along one section of shelves the complete track history of Ives, 1902 to 1930, containing O, number 1 and standard gauge.

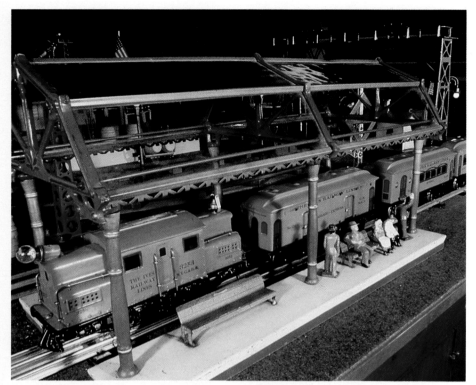

In the American Room:
Ives 3253 O gauge passenger set and Ives
glass dome station, circa 1924.

Voltamp 2 gauge steamer of 1908 dwarfs
the rare Carlisle & Finch paper label
station, circa 1904.

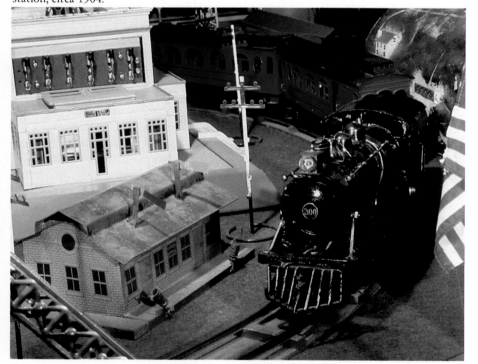

Finally, of course, there are Lionel
and American Flyer, with choice
standard gauge pieces represented
until 1940.

There are removable ¼-inch high
steel rods placed at close intervals
along the outer edges of all the
shelves. Known as "earthquake
guards" to California collectors, the
rods prevent trains from vibrating
off the shelves during tremors.

Kimball at first had all his trains in
one room with one layout, but in
1975 he acquired an entire collection of European items, compli-
menting his already extensive foreign collection, and he made
another room. Kimball, whose
round face is never more than a
moment away from an impish
grin, refers to the room with exag-
gerated elegance as the "Continental Annex."

"I like the European trains and
accessories better — the authentic-
ity, the workmanship," said Kimball. "They're hand painted, have
more detail than the American
stuff. Everything inside a car is
furnished. You can lift the roofs off
the stations and buildings and light
the candles if you want to."

The European layout contains four
loops, accommodating standard, O,
1 and 2 gauges. Kimball pointed to
a Marklin glass dome station and
shed, done in the Ives style for the
American market in 1914.

"In this depot, you can open the
doors and see tables and chairs and
benches. Marklin loved detail. In
Europe they were a little late getting electricity, so Marklin used
candles in a lot of their accessories.
There's a large freight station on
the top shelf over there. Compare
that to Lionel's version. With
Marklin you can lift the roof and
see all the details inside, slide the
doors and weigh your freight on
the scales. A kid could really play
railroad."

Ives 3217 red cast iron O gauge loco,
1912, with red 60 series cars under an early
122 **Tin-Truss** glass dome station, 1905.

Lionel 10 Interurban and trailer.

On the layout next to the glass dome station was a Marklin number 2 gauge clockwork train from 1900; on the next track was a number 1 gauge American-style clockwork with L.V.E. cars; on the O gauge track was a Marklin 0-6-0 with 8-wheel cars sitting next to a Fandor station. There is a Marklin tunnel with goats on the snow capped mountain and a sign that says, "Keep Dogs and Cats out of the Tunnel." There is a large number 2 gauge Marklin suspension bridge, very rare, from 1903, and a clockwork train from 1900 with cast iron wheels.

"Marklin at first made all their train wheels out of cast iron, then they realized that a heavy clockwork train didn't get enough trips around the track, so they changed their wheels to tin, which was much lighter," said Kimball.

Hovering above the layout in the Continental Annex, suspended by wires, are an old airplane and a dirigible. Kimball collects toys of all kinds, and one of his favorite things is a large Marklin battleship from 1908.

The walls contained more history, the complete history, in fact, of European-style toy trains, most made before 1914. Clockwork and steam powered O, 1, 2, and 3 gauge dominate the collection. The leading manufacturers represented are Marklin and Bing, with fine examples of Carette, Ernst Plank, Jean Schoenner, Karl Bub and Issmayer. There is a French Radiguet from 1875 and some English Stevens' Model Dockyard.

These early, obscure trains are identified with labels. Kimball considers his train building a kind of museum and often is the host to collectors and other interested railroad fans. But his collection is not the only thing to see at Ward Kimball's.

He also has a full-size railroad in his backyard.

The charm of Marklin in the European Room: ABOVE Brass 1 gauge American-style engine, with cowcatcher, and a rare Marklin 2524 tunnel. BELOW 0-4-0 2 gauge clockwork train, 1900, and a 1 gauge 4-4-0 electric, circa the 1920s, under a Marklin glass dome station of 1904. OPPOSITE TOP Marklin clockwork O gauge of 1906 and a Fandor glass dome station. OPPOSITE BOTTOM Marklin clockwork 1 gauge American-style loco in front of Marklin stations from the late 1800s and early 1900s.

Even in Ward Kimball's collection this is rare:
An Ives 40 in 1 gauge, 1904 to 1909.

It is a rather arresting sight to pull off Ardendale Avenue in a conventional-looking, up-scale sub-division of San Gabriel and see a big railroad train in the yard. A total of 900 feet of three-foot gauge track runs almost from the street, along the side of the house, to a three-stall engine house deep in the backyard.

It turns out that long before Ward Kimball collected toy trains, he was interested in the real thing. So in 1938, Ward and his wife, Betty, bought a 22-ton Baldwin 2-6-0 coal burning narrow gauge steam locomotive, circa 1881, from the Nevada Central Railroad. By 1943

the engine was completely restored to its original condition. Between then and 1960 the Kimballs acquired another engine, a wood-burning 9½-ton Baldwin, from the Waimanalo Sugar Company in Hawaii, and a passenger coach, a caboose, a boxcar, a gondola, and a cattle car. They added more track to accommodate the rolling stock. They built the engine house and an ornate Victorian station that Kimball initially filled with railroadiana and his toy trains. When the train collection grew too large he had to design the 60-foot building for the toy trains. The Kimballs call all this the Grizzly Flats Railroad.

The real thing — Kimball's 3-foot gauge locomotives. In the middle is a Baldwin 2-6-0 Mogul, named by Kimball "Emma Nevada" and made in 1881; at right is a Baldwin 0-4-2, named "Chloe" and made in 1883. Kimball has the oil can, his son, John, is "Chloe's" engineer. The hulk in front of the wagon, is a Kimball metal sculpture.

51

The Grizzly Flats Railroad: station, water tower, and engine house.

When the Kimballs settled in San Gabriel in 1940, it was an agricultural area, and theirs was one of the few homes around. In the 1860s their land had been a vineyard. In 1890 orange trees were planted, and it was into this grove that the Kimballs moved. Civilization has enveloped them and they are now surrounded by 13 neighbors. The encroaching urbanization has caused Ward to switch his engine operation from the old coal-burning Nevada-Central Baldwin to the cleaner wood-burning plantation loco, "Chloe."

Although encircled by suburbia, inside the Kimball's property line there is a feeling of 1940. Thick bushes and orange trees block off the outside world. The air is fragrant, the lovely, sweet-smelling orange blossoms tickling it. The orange trees are full of fruit, and oranges lie over-ripened on the ground. The railroad tracks run between the main house, which opens onto a swimming pool, and the toy train house. There are white alyssum along the tracks and a flower of strikingly simple prettiness, the California Poppy, a rich orange, which grows in the ballast where water is collected. Nearby is a bell from the old California mission trail, El Camino Real — "Mission San Gabriel Arcangel 26, San Juan Capistrano 31 Mission 11", a sign reads.

Deeper into the property the tracks go by the gingerbread depot with brick paving and an old green bench, and a baggage cart with trunks resting on it. There are a couple of old target switch stands, and three tracks branch past a 12-foot high, 100-year-old wooden windmill and into the engine house. The rolling stock sits on one side and a two-man hand car, maroon with yellow wheels and black handle, and a three-wheel velocipede stand nearby. Wood fuel is piled near the engine house, and railroad ties are stacked there too. Signs on the depot say, "Grizzly Flats Elev 492 Pop 5".
Obviously, a man has to have a deep and enduring interest in

trains to live amid all this. Kimball's interests, as well as his talents, are deep, enduring and varied.

Ward Kimball was born in 1914 in Minneapolis and very early showed a precocious talent for art and a fascination with trains, drawing his first choo-choo train when he was three years old. When he was six his parents, financially strapped, had him stay for a year with his widowed grandmother in a downtown Minneapolis hotel, the Hastings, where he was allowed to draw freely on hotel stationery and ride the trolley lines with his white-haired, adventurous grandmother. He collected street car transfers and drew, for hours on end, yellow trolleys with russet red roofs.

Soon after he moved back home with his folks, the family moved to Ocean Park, California, where he began drawing in earnest in fifth grade and when he was 11 took a correspondence course in cartooning. At about this time he received his first electric train, an Ives O gauge 3200 set and a tin Toonerville trolley. During his four years of high school he also attended art school, the tuition for which was provided by his early patroness, his grandmother. Despite the double curriculum, he graduated with honors from high school and completed the art course at the same time. He also learned to play the trombone. In 1932, at the height of the Great Depression, he received a scholarship to the Santa Barbara School of Art, a presitgious institution, where he worked as the school janitor and designed murals in downtown bars for jugs of wine or whatever else they could afford. Kimball had planned, upon graduation in 1934, to go to New York to become a magazine illustrator, but along the way he became impressed with the animated art work being done by Walt Disney. He drove his rheumatic 1924 Chevy coupe to the old Disney

Portrait of the artist as a young man, with "Casey Jr." for the movie, "Dumbo." RIGHT Jimmy Cricket, a Kimball design for "Pinocchio."

Hyperion studio in Hollywood, where the receptionist told him to leave his portfolio and they would contact him. Kimball explained that he didn't have enough gas to make another trip and asked if they would please look at his samples while he waited. Feeling sorry for the kid, someone took his work directly to Walt Disney's office, where an answer came back quickly: Ward Kimball, clearly a young man of promise, could start work the following week.

Kimball worked his way through apprenticeship in animation. He became an assistant animator, doing simple bits of secondary action, such as a flower waving in the wind, and then became a junior animator, working directly with the director doing fill-in scenes of less importance, like some angry bees chasing Donald Duck.

"These were exciting times," said Kimball. "Walt Disney and Mickey Mouse had become world famous. I was learning the craft and having fun."

Kimball worked on Walt Disney's first feature length film, "Snow White," a huge success that was followed by "Pinocchio," for which Disney made Kimball the supervising animator in charge of developing Jiminy Cricket.

"I managed to design a character with an egg-shaped head, no ears and a minature man's body," said Kimball. "Nobody seemed to mind that the cricket was no longer an insect."

One of Kimball's favorite Disney features is "Dumbo," which he calls "one of the tightest little pictures I ever worked on." From its inception to the final preview very few scenes were changed and it was finished ahead of schedule and under budget.

"I had the choice assignment of animating the black crows sequence, where these dancing, singing birds convince Dumbo that he can fly by using his big ears."

ABOVE Marklin clock-
work in 2 gauge, 1900,
and the rare Marklin
suspension bridge.
LEFT The Hubley ele-
vated railway, 1893, with
double clockwork motors.
Made of malleable steel
and cast iron.

A winter scene featuring a Marklin 1 gauge clockwork loco, 1898, with the American-style cowcatcher, and a Bing litho Ford Model T. Kimball has created a number of such scenes for covers of train magazines and for TV commercials.

It is a great sequence, considered a classic example of Disney animation. Kimball, the train buff, also designed the famous circus train in "Dumbo", which was pulled by the "Casey Jr." locomotive.

Kimball worked on most of the well-known Disney projects, including "Cinderella," for which he designed Lucifer, the cat, and the heroic little mice. "I based my design of Lucifer on a crazy-looking cat we once owned that had six toes and a perpetual sneer on his face." He created another cat for Disney in "Alice in Wonderland" — the slow moving, menacing Cheshire Cat — as well as Tweedle-Dee and Tweedle-Dum and the Mad Tea Party.

In 1952 Kimball turned to directing. He co-directed the first 3-D cartoon, "Melody," and followed that by directing the first Cinemascope cartoon, "Toot, Whistle, Plunk and Boom," which combined wide-screen action gags and stereophonic sound. It won him the 1954 Academy Award for best animated film. That was the year after Frank Sinatra won his Academy Award for best supporting actor in "From Here to Eternity." Both Kimball and Sinatra, although they don't know each other, belong to a West Coast train club called the Toy Train Operating Society, thus giving that organization the highest percentage of members who have won Academy Awards of any toy train club in the world.

Kimball won a second Academy Award in 1969 for an 18-minute cartoon-live action feature he created called "It's Tough to Be a Bird."

Kimball, whose pride in his work has never intruded upon his sense of the absurd or his zest for fun, said about his second Oscar: "It was a real thrill to pick up that award on national TV — wearing a paisley velvet suit with a pink shirt and a purple bow tie."

When Walt Disney was planning Disneyland in the mid-1950s, he decided to advertise the project through a weekly television show that would feature on alternate Sundays the four themes of the

LEFT A close-up of the Marklin large glass domed station containing an Issamayer 1 gauge locomotive of 1910. OPPOSITE Another view of the Continental Annex.

park — Adventureland, Frontierland, Fantasyland, and Tomorrowland. There was a vast backlog of films and cartoons in the Disney archives to supply the needs of the first three themes, but there was nothing for Tomorrowland. Kimball had been following a series of articles in *Colliers* magazine co-authored by Wernher von Braun, the scientist who pioneered rocketry.

"I thought these articles would be ideal to bring to life as hour-long Tomorrowland shows," said Kimball. "Of course, none of us realized how prophetic these four shows were to become: 'Man in Space,' 'Tomorrow the Moon,' 'Mars and Beyond,' and 'The Spy in the Sky.'"

The shows were informative and entertaining, with touches of the Kimball humor. Before the Russians launched Sputnik in 1957, President Dwight D. Eisenhower asked Walt Disney for a print of "Man in Space" to familiarize the Pentagon with the rudiments of a space program. In 1968, on the day Apollo 8 first circled the moon, Ward Kimball received a telephone call. It was Wernher von Braun.

"Well, Ward," he said, "it looks like they're following our scripts."

Looking back on the Tomorrowland shows, Kimball considers them "the creative high point of my career. The predictions that we made have all been coming true." Kimball's professional responsibilities never prevented him from pursuing other interests. He is a pilot, although he doesn't fly anymore. All the little airports that once dotted the San Gabriel Valley are gone now, replaced by tract housing and shopping malls. Of course he collects, all kinds of things, including jazz records. Some other artists at the Walt Disney studios were also collectors and some, like trombonist Kimball, were musicians. They began getting together in the late 1940s for noon time jam sessions. In 1949 Kimball organized a dixieland jazz band he named the "Firehouse Five Plus Two." The name was not inappropriate. Near the railroad track on Kimball's property is a small building — he calls it the firehouse — containing three old fire fighting vehicles from the turn of the century. The Firehouse Five Plus Two quickly became one of

the most successful recording groups of the time. From 1949 till 1970 they recorded 12 albums, their biggest success coming in the 1950s when, as Kimball says, "You could drive across the country and there would never be a time when you would not hear one of our records on one of the stations." The Firehouse Five often played in parades, riding along on Kimball's 1914 American La France hose and pumper truck.

"The band was always just a happy hobby," said Kimball. "But it made Walt Disney very proud that he had such versatile artists working with him."

Ward Kimball retired from Disney in 1972, at the age of 58. Ward and Betty's three children were long grown and embarked on their own careers. The Kimballs became world travelers and Ward collected trains and toys, worked on the Grizzly Flats Railroad, and generally had a fine time in his early retirement. Well, not complete retirement. In 1982 Walt Disney World in Florida opened its EPCOT Center, which included a

General Motors pavilion called World of Motion. One of the attractions at the pavilion is a 14-minute journey through the history of transportation. It involves the use of computerized figures and other objects with sound, animation and electronics. The transportation journey was designed by Ward Kimball, who for three and a half years oversaw every aspect of its planning and construction.

Kimball's earliest interest in toy trains was as a modeler. After joining Disney in 1934, he would go out on weekends to railroad yards and measure full-size trolleys and railroad rolling stock so he could make scale models of them. There were no kits in those days. He remained a scale modeler for a few years, with the normal disdain

modelers have for tinplaters, right up until he bought his real Baldwin locomotive.

"I lost interest in modeling once I was running my own full size railroad."

And then, gradually, his sense of history and attraction to antiques led him into collecting toy trains and ultimately his double layout train building and invaluable collection.

Standing in the Continental Annex of his trainhouse, he smiled as he looked across the layout.

"I still get a kick out of coming into this room," he said. "Sometimes I'll be sitting around doing nothing in particular and a friend of mine will call and ask, 'Hey Ward, what are you doing?'

"'Just reading the paper.'

"'How about having a few beers and playing with your choo-choos?' he'll say.

"So then he comes over and we come out here in the two train rooms and we run trains until sometimes three in the morning."

Kimball was once asked what single thing from his collection he would take if the San Andreas Fault began to open and he had to escape in a hurry. He replied that he would probably prefer to be swallowed up with the entire collection.

"Remember the old saying," he said. "He who dies with the most trains wins."

Phillip Klopp
Easton, Pennsylvania

"My Goal Is To Entertain"

It is not by accident that the layout in the basement of Phil Klopp's house has a definite museum feel to it.

It is by design, and Phil Klopp was the designer.

Klopp, given the space he had and his own taste, decided to build not so much a layout, with one sweeping view, but, as in a natural history museum, a series of dioramas, each its own vignette.

"Space is utilized better, and the viewer is not barraged visually with everything at once," said Klopp, standing in the middle of the 25-by-40-foot room. "He can walk slowly around and see one scene at a time."

Klopp began to walk slowly around. A shelf, built against all four walls, looped the room. Extending four feet from the wall, it contained a striking succession of miniature scenes: a stockyard here, a circus there, a city street with three-story buildings, kids playing in the park, and a trolley running down the middle of the street.

In the circus diarama a parade passes under a repainted Lehigh Valley GP-7, with the 2329 Virginia rectifier in the background.

There was a fire, with smoke billowing, being fought near a railroad yard; a Hiawatha snaked out of a tunnel somewhere else; and, next to a Lionel paper boy hawking the news, a burlesque house, marquee lights blinking, was packing them in for the risque Miss Fanne Foxe. No matter that the paper boy was gigantic next to the burlyque customers.

"My goal is to entertain," said Klopp. "I don't place the same emphasis on realism the HO gauge scale modelers do — I mean they count rivets — but I still try to make the layout as realistic as possible. Lionel made toy trains and their stuff is not in scale — like the paperboy or the crossing gates — but they work well and the kids love them."

Klopp got the idea for his layout when he read a Kalmbach publication called "Creative Layout Designs." Having dioramas around the perimeter of the room appealed to him, but he wasn't sure about how the room should be entered. Shelves would be in the way on all sides. One way, of course, would be to have people simply crawl under the shelf, but usually some sort of hinged section is installed. Klopp decided to enter from the top, from the hallway upstairs.

"I considered having a stairway that would move up and down electrically so there would be no obstructions at all, but I settled on a spiral staircase."

The spiral staircase winds down from a room off the upstairs hallway to the center of the room. There are speakers in the ceiling dispensing authentic railroad sounds. Next to the base of the stairs is the control panel, from which Klopp operates four tracks that run through, behind, up or under the dioramas. Some of the scenes have more trains in them than others. The city scene, for instance, has no trains visible at all, only the trolley running back and forth. There is a fascinating integration of trains and scenery throughout.

The town by day and the town by night. ABOVE Some buildings are from scale model kits. Others are scratch-built and fashioned after buildings with which Klopp was familiar while growing up, such as the Richland National Bank (second from left), where his father worked for many years. BELOW The Bowser trolley is operated by optical sensors installed at each end of the line. When the trolley blocks the light, DC current is reversed and the trolley changes direction.

Perhaps the most interesting aspect of the layout from an operating standpoint is the employment of a catenary system to operate the electrics, including several handsome GG-1s.

The catenary system is modeled after a set Pittman sold in the 1950s to operate its Brill trolleys. Klopp duplicated the poles, using welding rods and K&S brass for the cross pieces. N gauge rail is used for the wire. To operate a GG-1 by overhead wire, Klopp removed the wire to the roller pick-ups and attached it to the lug

Phil Klopp created this fire scene by adding a Seuthe smoking unit to a brewery kit made by Heljan, a Danish manufacturer. The smoke unit creates the smoke, while a recirculating pump shoots the water. A flickering red light, representing flames, emanates from inside, a technique achieved by punching holes in a tin can, covering the holes with red cellophane, and then rotating the can around a light by means of a small electric motor.

Phil Klopp is one of the few tinplate operators in America who has a working catenary system for his GG-1s.

under the pantographs. Tension is maintained by keeping the wire about ½-inch lower than the extended pantographs.

"This is the third layout I've had with a catenary system and this one works best," said Klopp.

Phil Klopp has built a lot of layouts in his 40 years, making his first one when he was seven. It was crude, with boxes for stations and crumpled butcher's paper for mountains, but it showed imagination. And he learned. He grew up fascinated with trains in his hometown of Richland, Pennsylvania, through which the Reading RR passed. By the time he was 15, he had built and dismantled 10 layouts.

Klopp's favorite engine is the Reading 4-8-4, custom made from two Lionel 2046 steamers. Stack and cylinder smoke come from an American Flyer smoke generator in the tender.

A Lionel 2379 Rio Grande F-3 stops at a 415 diesel fueling station, while the 497 coal loader operates on another track.

O-scale Reading camelback, modified for 3-rail track. The mountain was made by stapling screening to wooden supports and covering with paper toweling dipped in Hydrocal. (see page 65, top photo). Plaster rock castings were applied, and then Rit dyes were sprayed on with Windex bottles.

The circus diarama holds great attraction for children. But Klopp sees toy trains playing a smaller part in the lives of future generations. "Kids today aren't waving to engineers or visiting their grandmothers by train. The toy train market will remain good for this generation, but after that it doesn't look good."

He became a probation officer in Philadelphia, married an airline stewardess, the former Linda Schuler, and continued his interest in trains, both real and toy. One day in 1976, while attending the big York, Pennsylvania Train Collectors' Association meet, he saw a sign that a fellow collector wanted to sell his hobby shop and retire.

"Three months later, Linda and I quit our jobs, sold our home, moved to Easton, and got into the hobby shop business. It was probably one of the most unusual purchases that ever came out of York."

Ten years later, Klopp and Linda have no regrets about buying the Hobby Hangout and Craft Center.

"Business has been good and we both like Easton. Besides, I get lots of good trains through the store." Klopp collects mainly postwar Lionel but he also likes the charm of prewar and runs much of it on his layout, the 15th he has built. Most of the engines on the layout are early postwar, although he mixes in a lot of Fundimensions rolling stock.

"They are lighter and roll much better. I can have some 25-car trains with no problem."

He said he does not build layouts with any detailed plans.

"I have general ideas, like in that corner will be the mountain, the town will go here and the roundhouse over there. I draw a rough track plan and make changes as I go along."

As he talked, there was a pleasant sound nearby, like a brook murmuring. It came from alongside the mountain, where a waterfall ran. Most modelers use colored resins to simulate water, but Klopp does not.

"A good job with resin looks more realistic than real water, but I like the sound of my waterfall."

The Klopps' plans for the future include a new home, designed to accomodate at least two layouts.

Two prewar classics — the Hiawatha and the UP M10000. Klopp keeps all his trains in working order, although some he does not submit to the rigors of operation. "What I do run are not in the greatest condition, which means if I have an accident I won't go crazy."

The 456 coal ramp and 397 diesel coal loader. Klopp uses Gargraves track except on grades, where he uses Lionel's 027 track. He considers the Gargraves railheads too narrow for good traction.

One would be postwar and one prewar — "a classic prewar built around a beautiful lake."

The postwar layout would incorporate new sound systems and electronic control units that might operate the trains by radio control. It would not be in the basement.

"I'd like to have it be part of our living space. For instance, one part of it would be in the corner of the living room."

Linda should be used to it. When she first met Klopp in Philadelphia, he showed her around his apartment.

It was the first time she had ever seen a grown man with a toy train layout.

ABOVE Early stage before mountains were covered with Hydrocal. BELOW Like all operators, Phil Klopp has derailments and foul-ups from time to time, but this one is intentional, part of a damage repair scene near the lumber mill.

Michael Kolosseus
Everett, Washington

Pure Gilbert with Artistic Sparseness

Michael Kolosseus does not like clutter.

"When every square inch is covered, you don't see anything," he said, standing at one end of his 60-foot-long layout.

Every square inch is definitely not covered on the Branford & Western pike. But every inch is carefully considered. Kolosseus believes a handsome, realistic layout is achieved by a careful composition of scenery, buildings, accessories and space. He has spent as long as a week deciding the right spot for something.

"The idea is to create an illusion. Scenery should be designed to make things look bigger, not smaller. We know the size of trees.

ABOVE The clean lines of Michael Kolosseus's layout abound with bridges. There are five of them, including three which span a sky blue river. The longest stretches eight feet over a gorge. BELOW Kolosseus built the long spans himself, using Erector set girders.

If you put a tree on a mountain, you subconsciously know immediately how big the mountain is. Same with telephone poles. We know the distance between telephone poles. If we are trying to create the illusion of a great distance between one point and another, we don't put a string of telephone poles along the side of the track."

There are no telephone poles on Kolosseus's layout; no trees on mountains. In fact, there are hardly any trees at all. There are tawny mountains, multiple tunnels, long parallel sections of track passing under high, lonely bridges.

The effect is that of trains stretching through the sparse landscapes of the Southwest or arid California.

Because Kolosseus approaches his layout with so much care for composition, the stark look he achieves is not unlike that of a Georgia O'Keeffe painting. Or the colorful trains drawn against simple backgrounds in American Flyer catalog illustrations.

For above all, that is what Michael Kolosseus's layout is —American Flyer. The challenge he gave himself was to see how realistic he could make his layout using only unaltered Gilbert products: no modifications, no scale-detailed or scratch-built structures, no new electronics. He even resisted using wide-radius curves. Everything had to be Gilbert-made, and he wanted to display all of their products on the layout.

"For me, the greatest compliment would be if I were told my layout looks like something the Gilbert Company would have made for their Hall of Science."

Although he was interested in trains as a child in Portsmouth, New Hampshire, where he was born 48 years ago, he did not start

Kolosseus has tried to achieve the look of the Gilbert Hall of Science. ABOVE The room dimensions: 30x60. There are 900 square feet of table area, 1600 sections of track, 67 switches, and 38 transformers. RIGHT The accessories, except for a few Kolosseus made himself from Erector parts, are regulation American Flyer, including the automated cattle car and pen.

ABOVE Night falls on the Branford & Western pike. All wooden structures on the layout were made by Minicraft for American Flyer. RIGHT Realism was not the goal in the selection of buildings. "I think it's a detriment if you get too realistic," says Kolosseus. "It's wrong to build a beautifully scaled structure, weathered and detailed, on a toy train layout. It makes the toy trains look ugly."

collecting Flyer until he finished graduate work at Oregon State University in 1969. Kolosseus and his wife, Nancy, eventually started their own mail order business specializing in American Flyer S gauge. Now an economics teacher at Everett Community College, Kolosseus left the mail order business in the mid-1970s.

By 1978 the Kolosseuses had bought a home large enough to build the layout he always wanted, a pure Gilbert display in a space 60 feet long with widths that vary from 12 to 30 feet. He built along the walls, leaving a center area open for viewing. An open grid consisting of 1x4s and 2x2s with 2x2 legs was constructed. The level areas were covered with ⅜-inch plywood. A ½-inch homosote soundboard was placed over the plywood. Mountains were made with hydrocal, and oil paints were used for coloring.

Despite his concern with composition and the illusion of distance, Kolosseus's main goal was not realism but the display of Gilbert products and the smooth operation of them. He feels that too much realism can sometimes be a detriment.

"You put a beautifully scaled structure, weathered and everything, next to a toy train, and it makes the train look ugly. When I made my highway, I just cut it out of white posterboard. I made no effort to make it look real.

"Just as the trains and accessories are symbols of the real thing, so my highway is a symbol of a real highway."

But lines and proportions are another thing. Even though certain items may only be symbolic, Kolosseus believes they can live with each other in optical harmony.

"Take twenty buildings and space them evenly apart and they don't

TOP Kolosseus thinks Gilbert didn't make enough accessories, so he has built some himself, using strictly Erector set parts. Two Kolosseus specials are a magnetic crane and a log loader. BOTTOM The Circus Train glides down a straightaway.

look right. Put them in groups of fours and fives and they look better because real buildings are not spaced evenly. One should be very selective about where and what he puts on the layout. Less is better."

Another area where spacial relationships are important, according to Kolosseus, is between track. Twelve inches can expand or contract greatly there.

"Put a river between two stretches of track and they could be a hundred miles apart. Put a building between them and they seem right next to each other."

Kolosseus has an automated system that runs ten trains smoothly and gracefully for visitors who just want to ogle. But when his train buff friends come over he switches to a manual system for serious operations.

"We start in the yard making up a train. Each car has a point of origin and a destination. There are seven towns. Cars have to be picked up and dropped off, loaded and unloaded. When you return you have a completely different train which should match a list of cars you are supposed to return with. Nobody's done it 100 per cent correctly, but we have fun trying."

To aid in maintenance, all wires are tagged and the various lines are color coded — red for main power, yellow for lights and accessories and black for the base rail. Track is seldom cleaned — the sliding pickup shoes do the job — but Kolosseus lubricates the engines on a regular basis.

In spite of his opposition to custom-made scale items for the Branford & Western (named, incidentally, for a diner built by Flyer), Kolosseus did do a little scratch building of his own. But he kept it pure Gilbert.

(continued on page 76)

The Silver Bullet is the train that made Kolosseus a Flyer fan. "As a kid I loved that engine. After that, the only thing that kept me from being 100 per cent Flyer was their couplers. When they went from link to knuckle, I was American Flyer all the way."

Kolosseus was tempted to use a reproduction rather than assemble an original American Flyer circus kit. Once assembled, the cardboard circus loses much of its collector's value. Kolosseus decided to keep the layout pure Gilbert and, although it pained him, used the original.

A common motivation of train collectors is wish fullfilment: the ability to do as an adult what one could not do as a child. BELOW A scene of a Mystic Station as it was pictured in the Gilbert "Pike Planning" booklet. "As a kid I would have given anything to have that scene on my layout," says Kolosseus. ABOVE No longer a kid, Kolosseus has the scene on his layout.

ABOVE The trees are from Gilbert panel sets. Sawdust, dyed green, is used for vegetation.
LEFT Kolosseus places his accessories with careful attention to spacial relationships, sometimes taking two weeks before deciding on the precise location for an item. In the foreground, the 785 coal loader.

Many collectors feel the North Coast Limited is the most beautiful toy train, of any manufacturer, made in the postwar era.

Kolosseus' Tips

1. Go slow. Repress the urge to get the trains running as soon as possible. Make a plan and follow it.
2. Assemble the bench work with screws so changes are easy.
3. Inspect track carefully.
4. Use half-sections of track at the beginnings of grades.
5. Make clearance checks with your biggest engine on track and scenery as you go.
6. Switches and accessories need maintenance. Place them where you can get at them.
7. Place accessories where they can be seen.
8. Uncoupling locations should be within easy reach.
9. No downhill grade in the freight yard. You won't be able to couple.
10. Color code the wires.
11. Leave open space. It will make your layout look bigger.

He didn't think American Flyer made enough accessories, so he made his own — solely out of Gilbert Erector Set parts. Among the Kolosseus-designed-and-created accessories are a rotary dump, milk can loader, culvert loader, turntable, log loader, and magnetic crane.

There is, however, one accessory Kolosseus will not put on his layout. It is a Flyer-produced item called "Cow on Track."

"I wouldn't allow that on my layout," said Kolosseus. "The cow's as big as an elephant. It's so out of proportion I don't want it even if it was made by Gilbert."

Kolosseus has an extensive American Flyer S gauge collection display on shelves surrounding the layout.

"A collection is never complete," said Kolosseus. "What is complete? Do you have all the variations? Paper? Original boxes? Prototypes? Dealer promotional items and displays? What about department store specials? No one has it all."

Michael Kolosseus looked then across his layout. The trains, some of the finest S gauge ever built, were running, evenly and comfortably. A red, yellow and silver Sante Fe Alco crossed a bridge, its bright colors in attractive contrast to the gold-brown mountains and muted, lean landscaping.

It looked like a layout the Gilbert Company would have made for their Hall of Science.

Another Kolosseus invention: a culvert loader made from Erector set parts.

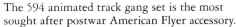

The 594 animated track gang set is the most sought after postwar American Flyer accessory.

76

TOP From certain perspectives the layout is reminiscent of an old American Flyer catalog. BOTTOM Kolosseus considered using Gargraves track for its wide-radius turns. "That would have looked better esthetically," he says. "But the challenge to me was taking the Gilbert stuff and making it look as good as possible."

"If we ever move, it will be into a bigger house, and I will build a bigger layout. The bigger the better. I'd make some improvements, like the overhead lighting, but I'd maintain my pure Gilbert approach," says Kolosseus. All the autos were made by either Manoil, Renwal or Tootsie Toy and were marketed as loads for American-Flyer flatcars.

Lionel Showroom
New York, New York

Close to the North Pole

It was not really that big.

Sixteen feet wide, thirty-two feet long. A good size, to be sure, 16x 32, but there are others in this book, in private homes, that are bigger.

But nothing looked bigger in the large eyes of the small children that stared at it through the years.

The Lionel Showroom layout.

Part of the aura of seeing it, of course, was that it was at Lionel. At the home office. The place where all the trains were made. They were not really made there, but the children didn't know that. What they knew was that this was Lionel and Lionel could put as much stuff as they wanted on the layout. They could make it. In December, this was as close to being at the North Pole as you could get.

The first thing you saw when you walked in was a 115 station and two rows of 156 platforms — five platforms in each row. See? They could put on as many platforms as they wanted. Between each platform Lionel added a section of fence so the fencing was uninterrupted the length of the platforms. See? Signs were attached to every other fence section. Four different signs were used — why not? They had plenty of them — Sunoco Dynafuel, Baby Ruth, Lionel Chemistry Lab, and Rival. A newsstand was located in the center of the row of platforms, closest to the viewer.

Two Lionel showroom layouts. ABOVE The T-rail, introduced in 1935, remained through 1948, although it was changed drastically in 1946. This photo was taken before the big change. OPPOSITE The O gauge layout introduced in 1949, and a favorite in the memories of many collectors. This view faces north, as you would see it coming off the street. In the foreground are the 156 platforms and the subway with the GG-1s. The inset is Joshua Lionel Cowen, the man who founded the Lionel Corporation. The photograph of the layout, and all the other pictures of the O gauge layout in this section were taken during the first six months after the layout was opened.

That scene actually describes the layout in the Lionel Showroom in 1949. The layout was a dynamic thing, changing in detail from year-to-year and in basic design five times in the 36 years it was displayed at the corporate head-quarters at 15 E. 26th St., New York, New York.

The first layout was built in 1926, in standard gauge. The layout remained a standard gauge one until 1936, when a layout featuring

This is one of the rare pictures taken of the back side of the mountain. The catenary system running along the track with the GG-1 was just for show. The trains drew their power from the track.

tunnel, a 437 power station, and a 444 roundhouse. Number 61 lamps ran on the edge of the main level and 94 high tension wires ran around the elevated level.

The T-rail introduced in 1935 was made for the scale model 700E Hudson, which was to be introduced in 1937. This layout was actually the net product of a process that had been set in motion in 1932 with an article on toy trains in *Fortune* Magazine.

The article had angered and embarrassed Joshua Cowen because it said "real railroadmen" played with scale models, not the tinplate stuff Lionel made. This, many people feel, was the genesis of Cowen's decision — along with a growing market of scale modelers — to produce the Hudson. And when the Hudson was introduced, a new layout was waiting for it.

The T-rail track remained through 1948, although the layout was changed in 1946, right after World War II. While the original had been a rather conventional display — a mountain, a tunnel, a village, various accessories — the 1946 version featured sweeping vistas. It was called the "Panorama," and included Niagara Falls, the Horse Shoe Curve in Pennsylvania, and Bride's Veil Falls in Yosemite.

The layout most Lionel fans remember — because of the age demographics involved — was opened in 1949. It was O gauge, and it lasted until 1957. Construction started right after Christmas Day, 1948 and was completed by the Toy Fair of February, 1949. The 16x32 rectangle was situated so that it could be viewed in a single sweep, uninterrupted by pillars or other obstructions. It had four main sections, or thematic groupings.

The first that greeted you off 26th Street was the passenger station

T-rail track was introduced. Information about the standard gauge layout is a bit sketchy, but some film footage taken in 1932 is probably typical of what was being displayed in the showroom.

The layout took up the same space as the later layouts, situated between the same six pillars. It had two main lines, one on the main level and one on an elevated level. A 400E headed a Stephen Girard set on the inside, elevated track. A

390 pulled Lionel-Ives transition cars on the outside track. Two 440 signal bridges, one on each of the long sides of the layout, spanned the track on the lower level.

At the near end of the room as you entered were some number 85 telephone poles, the 300 Hellgate bridge, a 438 switch tower, and a 840 power station. In the middle of the layout were a 921 scenic plot, a 128 terrace station, and a 77 crossing gate; at the far end was a 915

ABOVE The east
side of the layout
with the control
panel in the
foreground. RIGHT
The southwest side,
across from the
control panel and to
your left as you
entered the room.

OPPOSITE This is one of the few color photographs of the O gauge layout published. It appeared in *Esquire* magazine in December of 1953. All photographs of the layout are rather hard to come by, even the black and white ones. Most in this section appeared in *Toy Trains* magazine, published by Hal Carstens. Even Lionel had no pictures available if the public requested them. RIGHT The roundhouse and turntable were scratch-built by Frank Ellison. It is doubtful the turntable was ever meant to be operational. It was always pointed at the center stall. This photo was taken almost immediately after the layout opened in 1949, since the old furniture factory near the roundhouse was replaced during the first month by the modern plant shown in the color photo. Ellison also built the furniture factory.

scene. This was at the south end, which was 16 feet wide. The long, 32-foot sides of the rectangle ran away from the passenger station, along the east and west sides of the room. On your right, or east side, was the control panel, with four ZW transformers, lots of switches and buttons and the track diagram painted in thin white lines with red lights.

To the right of the control panel, away from the street, was the second major vignette of the layout, the engine terminal with turntable, roundhouse and storage tracks.

At the north end, the other narrow side of the rectangle, was the mountain. It was about 20 inches high.

On the west side, across from the control panel, was the last of the prominent vignettes, the joining of five main tracks, curving first in towards the center of the layout and then back towards the edge before rounding the bend into the passenger area. Scattered through this large open viewing area were a number of accessories, including the 164 lumber loader, the 97 coaling station and the 182 electromagnetic crane.

Besides the Lionel accessories, the layout contained a number of scratch-built structures, designed by the legendary modeler, Frank Ellison, of Memphis, Tennessee. These included a nicely detailed turntable, although probably not the roundhouse nearby. There were also five houses on the layout that came from Yank kits, and a church

and garage that were from Skyline kits. All buildings, both scratch- and kit-built, were carried over into the Super O layout except, unfortunately, the roundhouse and turntable.

The 1949 layout had six main lines on three levels. The main level had three main lines, two of which ran the circumference of the entire layout in full view. The third wound behind the roundhouse, entered a tunnel in the mountain, and reappeared to run parallel with the other tracks on the side of the layout opposite the control panel. The inside line on the main level had a long passing siding starting at the auto bridge on one side of the layout and ending at the turntable on the other side, near the control panel. This passed by the station platforms and created the

The pedestrian bridge in the picture above and the JLC factory in the photo on the left were both scratch-built. John van Slyke, the country's foremost expert on the Lionel O gauge layout, some day hopes to duplicate it in every detail, including the scratch-built structures. "I have all the track, accessories, and intimate knowledge," he says. "My only problem is — where in my house do I put a 16x32 foot layout?"

The O gauge layout from the southwest corner. The grain elevator in the foreground was one of the few structures that remained on the layout for its whole life, 1949-1957.

illusion that there were actually four mains on the main level.

On an elevated level was one main in a dogbone pattern — two loops connected by a straightaway. One loop ran around a village near the south end and the other ran through the mountain.

A lower level, about six inches below the main level, was somewhat like a subway. It had two mains. One stayed on the subway level for its entire loop, which was rather small, and appeared only at the large cutaway section below the 156 platforms. The second main line on the lower level rose to the main level, although it ran most of

its route out of view. This line appeared on the outside of the cutaway section, then disappeared again as it began a six-inch ascent to the main level just beyond the control panel. Here it reappeared briefly before rolling into a tunnel in the mountain. Emerging from the tunnel, it traveled in view past the 132 station, where it began its descent into the subway, passing out of sight near the 97 coal elevator. Both of the subway lines had GG-1s operating on them. The stretch of track from the mountain to the subway entrance near the coal elevator had a catenary system along it, as did the stretch on the other side between the control panel and the mountain. But these

were just for show. Both GG-1s received their power from the track.

This layout and all other showroom layouts before and after were designed to minimize operational hazards. Lionel wanted to display its products, and display them working, not breaking down. So they kept the operation simple while making the layout look more complicated than it was. All the loops were independent. There were not many switches, and none operated. They led to sidings and stretches of track that were never traveled. The big layout at Chicago's Museum of Science and Industry employs the same technique. It is full of fake switches and never-used running rails.

When the layout was redesigned with a ramp for displaying the pulling power of Magne-Traction, the GG-1 line climbed to the top level and ran around the mountain.

In the opinion of most tinplaters who paid attention to the Lionel showroom, the layout was at its best in 1949 when it opened for Toy Fair. Fortunately, most of the photographs that appeared later in *Toy Trains* magazine and in Lionel's books on model railroading were taken during the first six months the layout was in existence. Perhaps the country's foremost expert on the showroom is John Van Slyke of Wyckoff, New Jersey.

"I consider the first six months of the layout the best and every change after that diminished its original beauty," said Van Slyke, 46, who became interested in the showroom in early 1952, when *Toy Trains* began using photos of the layout for their centerfolds. He stared at the pictures, noticing every detail, and later that year his father took the 11-year-old Van Slyke to see the showroom. After that he visited the showroom whenever he could, studied the layout carefully, noticing every little change. He also began collecting photographs of it.

"My fondest memories of buying, receiving and operating Lionel date back to that period," said Van Slyke. "I feel it was Lionel's finest hour. Their quality, engineering, product line and catalogs were never as good before World War II or after 1952."

The layout built in 1957 had a much more plastic look to it than its predecessors. It featured a lot of elevated freeways — representing the advance of slot cars in Lionel manufacturing — and plastic-trestled railroad bridges.

List of items placed on the Lionel Showroom layout when it opened in 1949 (excluding track).

Catalog Number	Quantity	Description
022R	3	O Switch (right)
022L	5	O Switch (left)
26	8	Bumper
30	2	Water Tank
35	6	Boulevard Lamp
45	1	Gateman
64	2	Street Lamp
70	6	Yard Light
97	1	Coal Elevator
108	5	Highway Crossing Sign
308	1	Track Crossing Sign
308	5	No Trespassing Sign
308	4	Whistle Sign
308	6	Yard Limit Sign
115	1	Lionel City Station
132	1	Passenger Station
137	1	Stop Station
150	12	Telephone Poles
151	6	Semaphore
152	6	Crossing Gate
153	7	Block Signal
154	6	Highway Signal
156	11	Station Platform (with 9 Sunoco, 6 Baby Ruth, 7 Rival, and 7 Chem Lab signs)
164	1	Log Loader
182	2	Electromagnetic Crane
313	1	Bascule Bridge
314	10	Girder Bridge
317	2	Trestle Bridge
364	1	Lumber Loader
397	2	Coal Loader
711R	6	072 Switch (right)
711L	5	072 Switch (left)
ECU-1	1	Electronic Control Unit
RCS	12	Remote Control Track
ZW	4	Transformer

No matter which layout was in the showroom, however, Josuha Lionel Cowen was protective of it, sometimes even defensive.

There is a story that Louis Hertz, one of the earliest and best known of the toy train collectors, was looking at the Panorama, shortly after it opened. Cowen walked up to Hertz, a frequent showroom visitor.

"What do you think?" he asked, with the pride of a new parent. Hertz looked at the high, hilly landscaping.

"You can't see the trains," he said.

Cowen, offended that anyone would find fault with one of his marvelous creations, turned around without saying another word and walked out of the room.

Two views of the Super O layout,
which opened in 1957. The
control panel was now in the tower
above. Super O track was used,
but there was a strong emphasis on
cars and roadways. Lionel had by
this time begun to think about
selling slot cars and other items in
the hope of increasing sales, which
had been on a downward trend.

Bruce Manson
Lancaster, Pennsylvania

A Stroll Down Memory Lane

It is a toy train layout different from most others in the world. The central focus is not on trains, nor the track they run on.

It is on dozens of people doing everyday things that have nothing to do with trains, even though they might do them in close proximity of railroads.

"I tried to create a realistic landscape," said Bruce Manson, the creator of this workaday world, as he looked over his domain. "I have trains where trains would be in real life. Not all over. I'm happy with the results — a massive, busy cross-section of life that includes both urban and country scenes."

Manson, the editor of the *TCA Quarterly*, the official magazine of the Train Collectors Association, refers to the figures on his layout as "Dracula people." He has interchanged arms, legs and heads from different figures to create poses not available in store-bought items.

"Everyone is doing something, frozen in action," he said. "Gives each scene a meaning."

It is a massive layout, 30x40 feet, and every inch of it is covered with people and animals, buildings and houses, mountains and waterways, roads and streets, trails and track. There are scenes from rural and city life. The little people, in suspended animation, are all in action — putting up storm windows, mailing letters, haggling at garage sales, casting fishing lines, waving

Bruce Manson's layout is loaded with reminders of his life. ABOVE A custom-painted Northern Pacific 4-6-2 steams past a lighthouse which is similar to the ones on Cape Cod and Martha's Vineyard where the Mansons spent many summers.

flags. This is not to say train activity is ignored. People board streamliners, brakemen signal engineers, watchmen climb towers.

But there is so much more: in a second-story window a model poses nude for an artist, while on a street corner a policewoman directs traffic, and down the block a man enters a diner, a priest leaves a church. The activity is bustling, almost frantic in places, a frozen rush hour where only the trains actually move but everything else appears as though it does.

Manson designed his own buildings and made them by "kit-bashing" or "cross-kitting," which means he used parts of more than one kit, and then weathered them with chalk. He views the layout as a sort of animated scrapbook.

"The buildings evoke memories — like the Carlyle Hotel I built after the one in Manhattan where my friend George Feyer used to play the piano. I have a music box under the hotel that plays Cole Porter, just like George used to play. Things that were important to me are on the layout. I have a Lord & Taylor department store because I used to work there, a model of the Gilbert Hall of Science, and Carmen Webster's Hobby Shop.

"Late at night I'll walk around the block [as Manson refers to walking around his layout], sip a drink and sort of relive my life."

Manson, 55, was raised on Long Island and had a standard gauge layout in the late 1930s, before the emphasis shifted to realism in toy trains. Then he switched to American Flyer O gauge and later to S because it was closer to scale than Lionel. It is still an S gauge world he oversees, a world for him that is almost Utopian.

"There's no crime, no graffiti, no pollution. Everyone's a Republican.

OPPOSITE The Carlyle Hotel in New York, New York where Manson's friend played piano at the Bettleman bar. A concealed music box plays Cole Porter. TOP Manson was at Gilbert Hall of Science the day they converted the layout to S gauge. MIDDLE Bruce was once in the real estate business. BOTTOM He was never in the investment business but the building's title attests to his sense of fun.

91

The whimsical world of Bruce Manson covers city, suburban, and country living.
ABOVE Suburban Manhassat is hopping with action. OPPOSITE TOP Manson is
one of the few layout builders who attempts urban scenes with multi-story structures.
OPPOSITE BOTTOM A country town, one of several western vignettes represented.

There's the Taft Hotel, the Theodore Roosevelt Station, the Eisenhower Plaza and the Nixon Jail."

Manson likes the sound of toy trains on the track, so only American Flyer roadbed separates the track from a plywood surface. The table is braced by 2x6s to insure it can support over 1,000 pounds of plaster on the mountains and a few real boulders. There is also a couple of hundred pounds of Manson, when he walks on top to make repairs. It was his wife, Anna, who insisted on using 2x6s, even though the carpenter felt that 2x4s would be adequate. The caution is something Anna has in common with the aide to Frank Sinatra, who also

is of the opinion that the most valuable item on a layout is a human being (see page 132).

Manson paints both rolling stock and engines to make road names he likes. One of his engines is a custom-painted version of a Southern Pacific Daylight. The former marketing manager of Fundimensions saw that engine once when he was visiting and was impressed.

"They won't admit it," Manson said with a smile, "but I know that's when they got the idea to make the Daylight."

Manson considers accessories too toy-like for his layout, and the only one he uses is the Flyer barrel loader. He has tried to keep every-

thing in scale, including the street lights, which are HO but have been lengthened to fit S gauge. A Lionel HO gauge banjo signal is next to a siding, in perfect proportion for S gauge, another indication of Lionel's lack of concern for proper size.

Manson can only operate one train at a time on each of the two main lines, but hidden on sidings under the mountains are ten more trains that can come out to the mains. To create the feeling of distance, he operates HO gauge half-way up the mountains and N gauge at the peak. He got the idea while driving through Donner Pass in the Sierra Nevada mountains on the way to San Francisco.

(continued on page 96)

Vacation areas, naturally, haven't been neglected in Manson's idyllic existence. OPPOSITE TOP Rustic streets lie against a wooded hillside. OPPOSITE BOTTOM Antiquing is very much in vogue in resort towns, and passengers aboard the SP Daylight get a good view of the antique shop. ABOVE and LEFT The Grand Hotel, at the foot of a hill, is a fine spot for fishing, boating, and catching a few rays.

ABOVE To create the illusion of height, Manson runs different gauges in mountains — S on the ground, HO in the middle, and N on top. Here, a Fleischmann HO railbus passes above an S gauge Daylight and freight. BELOW The real Greenwich, Connecticut, where the Mansons have relatives, was never busier than this.

"I saw an SP Daylight about 200 feet above. It looked like HO scale. Further away, I saw a freight entering a snow shed. It looked like perfect N scale."

This is the fifth operating layout built by Manson, who has had one in every house he has lived in since 1938. The biggest was the one he had when he and Anna lived in Reno, where Bruce sold real estate.

"Bruce called from Reno and said he had put a deposit down on a house," said Anna. "I asked how many bedrooms it had and about the kitchen. All he could tell me was that it had a 30x70 foot garage, big enough for a great layout. When I moved, I still didn't know if my new home even had a kitchen, a bath or any bedrooms. But I knew it had a 30x70 foot garage."

The Manson layout is on the second floor of a large, white barn which sits on a hill above their rumpled white farmhouse outside Lancaster. The first floor contains Manson's collections — Tootsie Toys and Marx besides American Flyer, of which he has one production example of everything made in S gauge. He regards his collection much the same as he does his layout, as snippets of his life easily accessible for review. He would not change anything.

"I know where every piece came from. Maybe everything is not mint, but it's at least very good. The memories are more important than condition. Like my New Haven electric: I bought it at Savoy in Manhattan. That was my first S gauge engine. I've used it on every layout I've built since the war. It's got some chips, but do you think I'm going to sell that engine for one in better condition?"

No.

Not Bruce Manson, that sentimental boulevardier, strolling past the Carlyle as Cole Porter music floats across the night air.

I've got you under my skin
I've got you deep in the heart of me

And that goes for chipped and scratched New Haven electrics, too.

LEFT Manson's layout is on the second floor of an old barn. On the first floor is his collection of toy cars, lead soldiers, and paper advertising. BELOW Anna Manson is very much involved in Bruce's train activities and has a layout of her own in another room in the barn. In the foreground is a Lionel streamlined passenger set converted into a circus train. In the background is the 1978 version of the Lionel Blue Comet.

Michael Primack
Lake Forest, Illinois

Real Railroad Operations Reproduced

When Michael Primack picks up the phone in the basement of his Lake Forest home, he always knows what the call will be about: toy train deliveries.

Michael Primack is not in the toy train business, nor does he own a hobby store. He is a dentist. The phone in his basement is part of his toy train layout. It rests on a cradle at a control panel near a little town and a big switch yard. On the other side of the layout, separated by a high mountain, is another control panel near another town. This panel also has a phone, which is connected to the phone at the first control panel.

With Primack at the controls of one panel and another operator at the controls of the other, the two keep in contact by phone and simulate the freight operations of a real railroad. They become dispatchers, ordering trains with specific consists from the switch yard, for instance, or from one town for

(continued on page 103)

The crowded main switch yard on Michael Primack's layout. In the middle, two empty culvert cars are waiting to be picked up. The pickup and delivery procedure is pictured on the following two pages.

Primack, left, at the control panel near the switchyard, receives a call from his son, William, right, at the panel across the mountain near the town of Heaven. William places an order for two full culvert cars, a loaded lumber car, an empty hopper, and an empty tank car.

A switcher finds the culvert cars shown on page 99. Primack uses standard Lionel uncoupling magnets with his Gargraves track. He cuts an inch out of the center rail, removes four ties, and secures the electro magnet to the layout surface. A bypass wire reconnects the center rail, and the magnet is wired to a control button on the control panel.

The Lionel culvert loader in operation. The culvert cars have now been joined with the lumber, hopper and tank cars to form the consist bound for the town of Heaven. They will next be taken to a siding to await a mainline freight.

LEFT An Erie-Lackawanna F-3, part of the mainline freight's ABA unit, picks up the consist, the culvert car in the lead. Before it can get on line, however, it must wait the passage of a Chessie passenger train, its red, yellow and gray colors a blur as it streams by. BELOW Once in the Heaven area, the cars are unloaded in sequence. The tanker, the last car in the consist, is dropped off first. The caboose is left by a refinery siding while the rest of the cars are backed in and the tanker uncoupled. The culvert car, the first to be picked up in the switch yard, will be dropped off last.

The custom-made switches by Steve Brenneisen are what allows Primack to lay his track so close together. LEFT A double crossover switch near the town of Heaven. BELOW The main switch yard, close to the automatic culvert loader.

delivery to the other town. The mountain that separates the two towns runs from the floor to the ceiling and is situated so the dispatchers cannot see each other. The problem is to assemble the train consist in a proper sequence, so the cars can be uncoupled as they reach their destinations — the coal cars at the coal mine, the lumber cars at the lumber mill, and so on.

Complicating matters is a Union Pacific passenger train that is continually running on schedule on the main line. The operators have to do their switching, moving, and uncoupling of freight cars without running into the passenger train. And nothing is done by hand. Every engine and car is moved without touching it.

The whole operation of Primack's layout simulates very closely the operations of real railroads. That is by design and is the whole theme of the 25x25 foot layout.

Primack originally had a more conventional layout in the basement — all Lionel equipment and Plasticville structures. It had 072 switches and curves and independent loops. He was happy enough with it, but there was something gnawing at him.

"I had some kind of vague idea that I wanted to simulate real railroad operations, and you just couldn't do it with Lionel," said Primack one night while sitting at the control panel overlooking the switch yard. "One problem was the switches. To have a switch yard you need a lot of switches and a lot of track side-by-side. The closest you can get track side-by-side with Lionel switches is seven inches from center rail to center rail. That is, you put a piece of curved Lionel track into the switch and then put in straight track to get it running parallel with the other straight track, and the two sets of straight track will be at least seven inches

The pine trees were made from Scentree kits. Circles of steel wool were glued to a tapered dowl which had been painted black, then stained gray to simulate bark. The steel wool was sprayed with matte medium and sprinkled with green foam. There are over 200 trees on the layout. Each took about two hours to make.

The control panel for the main switch yard. In the upper left hand corner of the picture is Lionel's 350 transfer table. The control for the transfer table is in the upper left hand corner of the panel.

A mixture of matte medium and water, about a 10 to 1 ratio, holds the ballast in place. "This mixture is better than Elmer's glue and water because it dries to a flat finish," says Primack. "Elmer's mixture dries glossy." Primack was influenced by Dave Frary's book *How to Build Realistic Model Railroad Scenery*.

apart from center rail to center rail. That's too far apart.

"Since we're talking about quarter-inch scale, that means there would be, in real life, 28 feet between tracks. If you try to build a switch yard with a lot of parallel tracks you need a lot of space and it doesn't look right. In real roads you can barely walk between the cars. In a yard made with Lionel track and switches there would be about 25 scale feet between cars. It looks terrible and is impractical because you would need a board about 70 inches wide to hold ten parallel tracks."

Primack still had his yearning for a dispatcher-style layout in the back of his mind one day in October of 1983 when he attended a train meet in DuPage County, Illinois. He saw a display of custom switches by Steven Brenneisen —Y switches, curve switches, three-way switches and standard right and left switches. Brenneisen's switches would allow parallel tracks to rest as close as 3¼-inches from one another, center rail to center rail. This meant Primack could make a layout with as many as 15 parallel tracks on a 48-inch wide board.

Primack made a deal with Brenneisen: he would buy a large number of switches from Brenneisen if Brenneisen would design a layout for Primack's 25x25-foot room. Brenneisen agreed, and the planning began. Primack wanted to incorporate good scenery with Gargraves track and Brenneisen's custom-made switches. All loops would be interconnected.

Primack was well on his way to having his long-envisioned layout that would simulate a real railroad operation, but there still remained one major obstacle.

Michael Primack did not know anything about how real railroads operate.

A trestle bridge spanning a deep river gourge offers the kind of dramatic vista usually associated with HO layouts. Primack achieves the scale look in O gauge by building his mountain from the ceiling all the way down to the floor, not stopping at table height like most O-gaugers do.

The other side of the mountain. A Santa Fe geep next to Lionel's 164 log loader. A Union Pacific passenger train speeds over the bridge in the background.

He began doing research. Each weekend he drove around the Chicago area and studied how switch yards operate. He drove downstate, to towns like Kankakee, Coal City and Chebanse. He watched them build trains, watched how the local trains mixed with the express trains on the mainlines, and how dispatchers ordered trains with a specific consist to be delivered at a certain time. He learned about double-ended yards (yards with entrances and exits), stub-end yards (yards with entrances but no exits), open sidings (sidings that lead back to the main line), and stub-end sidings (sidings that end with track bumpers).

Using a grain car as an example, this is part of what Primack found out about how real railroads operate:

The owner of a grain elevator in Chebanse calls a local dispatcher and orders an empty grain car; at the same time he requests that a loaded grain car be picked up. The Chebanse dispatcher calls a dispatcher in Kankakee, which is closer to Chicago. The Kankakee dispatcher locates an empty grain car in Chicago and places his order. Orders from all over are coming to the Chicago yard, and the dispatcher there assembles blocks of cars, including several for the southern Illinois area serviced by the Kankakee yard. These blocks are made into a mainline freight in Kankakee, and the freight heads for southern Illinois, dropping the blocks of cars off at sidings along the way.

The grain car is dropped off at the Chebanse siding, along with other cars designated for that area. All of these cars are in the proper order; they will become part of a local freight and dropped off at each business as it comes up along the track. The grain car is dropped off at the grain company's siding, and

Two views of the town of Heaven, so named because that's where Primack's wife, Eileen, says he is when he is playing with his trains. ABOVE The downtown area, with the Lionel newsstand, one of several out-of-proportion accessories Primack keeps on the layout. LEFT The outskirts of town, with many of the same Plasticville buildings Primack had when he was a kid. He keeps the Plasticville buildings and the accessories on the layout because of their nostalgic value. Some day he might replace them with weathered and detailed buildings, he says, but then again he might not.

Primack normally has wood paneling on the walls behind the layout. Here, he borrowed a background with painted renderings of hills and mountains. He now plans to install scenic backgrounds.

the car loaded with grain is picked up, taken to the Chebanse siding, and then hauled up to Kankakee to await a main line freight to take it to market in Chicago.

Using Brenneisen's switches and Gargraves track, Primack has simulated this operation on his layout. He takes the controls of one panel, and a fellow train enthusiast takes the controls of the other. They order cars, make up trains, deliver cars, and pick up cars — all on schedule. They use a fast clock in which ten minutes equals one hour.

Primack has two main lines, a double-ended switch yard, and numerous industrial sidings. All are connected. Power is supplied by two ZWs at each panel. One panel

controls the switchyard and accessories in the switchyard. The main panel controls the two mainlines and the accessories along the mainlines. Two LW transformers are located under the layout. They control the Tenshodo switch machines, the lights for the switches, and some accessories.

The large town located near a brewery is named Heaven. A smaller town in a far corner is Hillside. Much of the layout runs along the walls and is separated from the center mountainous area by viewing aisles. The mountain creates the illusion of distance between the towns.

The table level of the layout is 36 inches. Brenneisen feels the best

height for a layout like Primack's would be close to eye level, so you could get the same track-eye view you get with real trains. But a layout has to be accessible for repairs and changes, and 36 inches is a more practical height.

"Operationally, the layout is finished," said Primack. "It's fun and exciting. It operates just like real trains operate. Now I can enjoy running the trains and concentrate on the detailing. The layout will never be finished, but the key is that while I add detail I can operate the way I want. I can super-detail forever. Operationally, I am very satisfied.

"In the space I have I couldn't have done it better."

Union Pacific and Lackawanna F-3s coming out of the mountain.
Primack couldn't find tunnel portals that were wide enough to
accommodate two sets of tracks, so he cut single portals in half and
spliced in extra sections to reach the required width.

Stan Roy
Glenview, Illinois

Synchronized Relays, Record Performance

In the basement of his two-story Georgian home, within earshot of the Glenview Naval Air Station and the Milwaukee Road commuter tracks, Stan Roy operates 27 different trains on six loops and three levels, automatically and all at the same time.

It may be a world's record for simultaneous operation.

"Some guys have bigger collections, others have bigger layouts, but I have never read or heard of anyone who can run as many trains as I can at one time," said Roy one spring afternoon while watching his trains operate at maximum efficiency. His eyes were bright and darting, like those of a juggler with 27 crystal plates in the air.

Roy uses a system of over 200 relays that allows as many as seven trains to run on a single loop, all trains stopping and starting automatically while maintaining safe intervals. Other trains on other loops pass crossovers and switches in front of the trains on the first loop, but no train ever runs into another. The system, once activated, requires no assistance from the operator.

Roy, 43, began his unprecedented project in 1977 by having a new house designed with an especially large basement. He constructed a table out of 2x4s and ¾-inch plywood, 36 feet long and 9 feet wide. An addition — 5 feet wide and 50 feet long — was added later.

The heart of the matter: A busy intersection with the inset picture showing two of the relays that allow Stan Roy to operate 27 trains at one time. They are double pole, double throw, 12 volt electrical relays made by the Guardian Company. They cost about $18.

111

For Roy's plan to work, it was crucial that all the trains on the same loop maintain the same speed at all times.

"With a Lionel ZW transformer, if you stop or start more than one train at a time, the others will surge and go so fast they will probably jump the track or they will slow to a crawl," he said. To operate five trains on a loop requires about 8 amps delivered on a continued basis (each Lionel motor draws about 1½ amps). This was beyond the capacity of Lionel transformers, so Roy installed industrial 30 amp DC power supplies capable of delivering a constant voltage regardless of current draw.

While solving the problem of surging, another was created. A short circuit would cause all 30 amps to go directly to the spot where the short occurred.

"I welded quite a few wheels to the track," he said. Roy solved this problem by installing electronic circuit breakers that trip in microseconds.

Although Lionel motors will operate on DC without modifications, DC also activates whistles and horns. Roy ran the DC on reverse polarity to stop the constant din.

Even with regulated DC power, however, all engines did not run at the same speeds.

"The running speed of each engine had to be controlled. Some engines run faster, pull better and stop quicker. I installed diodes in series with the motors. A diode will drop the voltage six-tenths of a volt. Some engines required six diodes, others required one or two."

Maintaining contact between the engine pickups and the track topped Roy's list of priorities.

ABOVE Roy's passenger station is hopping, day or night. "My ultimate goal is to buy the Lionel Company," says Roy. "Then I guess I would have all the trains I would ever need." LEFT A Southern Crescent crosses a bridge after emerging from the mountain.

LEFT A frequent sight when you're running 27 trains at once: the crossing gates are down.
BELOW A Southern Pacific Daylight passes over an Alton Limited. Both sets are prized.

The bascule bridge has a reputation as an erratic performer but Stan Roy found the opposite to be true. "I was told the bascule bridge would give me grief" recalls Roy, "but I've never had any problems and it's going up and down all the time." To improve performance on some of the other Lionel accessories, Roy has replaced the original Lionel motor with a direct current motor.

"I learned with my first layout that if contact is lost even momentarily, relay chatter can cause a waiting train to crash into one on the crossover."

To prevent such accidents, Roy installed four different main bus wires, one each for the track, ground, relays and accessories. The wire and track connections were soldered for the best contact, and everything was secured with screws. To further improve contact, Roy had all the wheels on his rolling stock nickel plated.

"This was a big job. I had to take all the wheels and axles off and take them to a plating company. The guy thought I was nuts when I walked in with two thousand toy train wheels and a thousand axles."

Roy did not want all the trains operating on the same loop to follow the same path.

"On the average loop, I have eleven places where the train has a choice to go either right or left. I wanted them to alternate direction each time they crossed a switch. Otherwise, they would look like one long train."

He installed sequence relays at each switch, but maintaining contact so the switch wouldn't change in the middle of a train proved to be such a serious problem it almost forced Roy to abandon the project. He was having crashes and derailments and became obsessed with solving the problem.

"I'd be at dinner with my wife and friends, and all I could think of

were new ways to lock a switch. If something occurred to me I couldn't wait to get home. Then I'd kiss my wife good-night and race downstairs to see if my new idea would work."

Roy tried different methods including latching relays, but nothing worked. It took six years to come up with a system that would hold the switch securely in one position.

"Magnets were the answer. I put a magnet on each engine. The magnet activated a magnetic switch which would trigger the sequence relay."

With that problem at long last solved, Roy was ready to present himself with a new one, a grand finale conundrum.

Roy outfitted this prewar 0-6-0 switcher, one of his favorite engines, and caboose with postwar knuckle coupler trucks. The warped roof walk on the caboose, caused by impurities in the metal, is a common problem with prewar die-cast equipment.

"Lionel was bringing out these seven-foot passenger sets like the Norfolk & Western, Southern Pacific Daylight and New York Central. I wanted a loop for those passenger trains and a big station where as one passenger train pulled in, it would slow down and stop and another would pull out."

Roy, an electronic whiz who is co-owner of a cassette tape duplicating company, remembered how much time he spent solving the switch problem. This time he assigned the company's top technician to come up with an answer. Roy complicated the problem by insisting that two freight trains should also run on the loop, but without stopping at the station, although they would blow their whistles each time they

approached. The technician designed an intricate resistor-capacitor, charge-and-discharge timing circuit which allowed the advance of a stepper relay, slowing one train while simultaneously starting another.

The technician worked so long on the project that Roy's partner put a "Lionel Research Department" sign over the technician's work area. But his partner, Bill Benett, also became involved, said Roy.

"My partner became fascinated with toy trains and got into LGB. He built a layout and everything. Now he is more understanding."

Roy's wife, Janice, and brother-in-law, Bob Richmond, a design architect, landscaped the layout. While

most motive power is from the Lionel production of the mid-70s and after, almost all the accessories are from Lionel's postwar era. Roy has replaced Lionel's erratic vibrator system with a brushless DC motor, resulting in a quieter and more efficient operation.

Stan Roy continues to buy every major set Lionel makes. This led to the construction of a second level on his layout and then, in 1986, to a third. The third level stands 24 inches above the lower level and operates up to ten trains.

"Either Lionel has to go out of business or I'm going to need more space," said Roy, eying with open longing the space in the basement

(continued on page 121)

Fifty years of Hudsons.
ABOVE In the
foreground, the 782
Boston and Albany,
made by Lionel in 1987,
and in the background,
the 5344 New York
Central, made in 1937.
LEFT The 5344, with the
Lionel catalog number
of 700E, was the first
Hudson Lionel built and
was a full-scale, highly-
detailed model.

ABOVE Some of Lionel's
most valuable collector's
items. From the top: the
Norfolk & Western J; the
new Boston & Albany Hud-
son; the 1964 version of the
Hudson; the 1950 version;
the 700E with Rail Chief
car; the 0-6-0 prewar semi-
scale switcher; the Hiawatha; and the hardest to find
of all Hudsons, the 763 in
gray with gray coal tender.
The old trains are not Roy's.
Some friends brought them
over for the fun of watching
them all run at the same
time. RIGHT A prewar
switcher in front of a Plasticville log cabin. One of
Roy's relays is hidden
inside the cabin.

The passenger terminal area. LEFT and BELOW An elite fleet awaiting individual departure times. Through Roy's automatic relay system, as one passenger train pulls into the station, it slows to a stop and another train pulls out. In the meantime, freight trains go by, but don't stop; they only toot their whistles.

ABOVE On an open stretch the Southern Crescent passes the 132 Lionel station. LEFT Roy has a reproduction of a prewar Lionel station at the center of his passenger terminal. "I think reproductions are great," says Roy. "You can get accessories brand new without paying those outrageous prices."

ABOVE Lionel
Scale — the Hudson
and the 0-6-0
switcher. LEFT
Three Hudsons
from earlier eras.
OPPOSITE The
story of Stan
Roy's layout:
relays, switches
and trains working
in endless
synchronization.

now occupied by a family rec room. The Roys have a girl in college and a boy in high school.

Although he has a valuable collection, mainly of Fundimensions Lionel, Stan Roy is above all an operator. "I never wanted to display trains on shelves and kiss them good night every night. Everything I own has to be on a siding on the layout with the capability of getting to the main line.

"I firmly believe nobody has accomplished what I have accomplished. When I travel, I never leave a town without visiting a hobby shop. I talk with the guys. They all have this rare train and that rare train. But can they operate? Can they put their trains on the track? I want people to know I operate my trains — all my trains."

Tom Sefton
San Diego, California

Youthful Dreams Fullfilled

Tom Sefton, when he was growing up in the 1920s, was the archetypical poor little rich boy.

Although his father was the wealthy owner of a San Diego bank, he was determined not to spoil his son.

"As a young boy I didn't have a lot of toys," says Sefton. "I must have had a latent desire for toys."

The desire was not always so latent. Sefton went to a military grade school, where after lights out he would crawl under the blankets with a flashlight and read the Lionel catalogs, which displayed the great standard gauge trains of the era.

So it was that when he grew up and was himself in the banking business, he began to satisfy the cravings of the little boy that still resided in the man.

The boy apparently demanded a heap of satisfaction.

Tom Sefton's Lionel standard gauge layout, in terms of numbers of rare pieces, is probably the finest in the

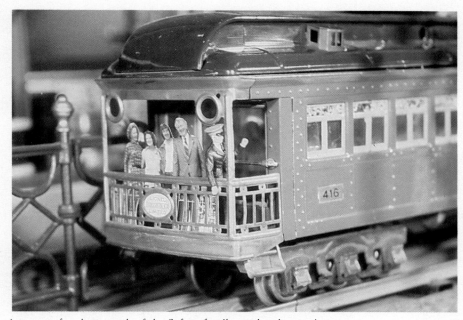

A cutout of a photograph of the Sefton family on the observation deck of the New York state car. The picture was taken while the family stood on a real railroad car — the one Tom Sefton owns.

world. He has at least one of every piece Lionel made in their classic period, 1923 through 1939, except the nickel-trimmed 400E Blue Comet steamer.

"I'd have to buy the whole set to get the engine and I don't want to do it," says Sefton, who apparently feels he doesn't need any more of the passenger cars that go with the

400E. He already has 30 state cars and fourteen Blue Comet cars (five trimmed in nickel). They compliment his 200-series freight cars, of which he has 130. For that matter, he already has eight 400Es.

He can run two trains at one time on his almost 600 feet of track. He uses only state cars, 418-series cars and 200-series freights on the

ABOVE In the foreground, some of the 30 state cars and dozens of 200-series freight cars in Sefton's collection. The background is a dealer display panel. LEFT The rare 408E in two-tone brown. The station is decorated for Christmas.

layout. The consists vary, but a typical one might be two 381s pulling seven state cars or a 408 pulling ten 213 cattle cars and ten 214 box cars — and a 217 caboose, naturally. Or perhaps he might use two 390s pulling thirteen 218 dump cars and a caboose.

Sefton's layout lines the perimeter of a packed second floor train room of his red-brick house in San Diego. Tucked under the eaves, the layout runs along three sides of the room. Every Lionel standard gauge accessory is represented, and a few O gauge. The only things on the layout that aren't Lionel are three Ives water towers.

"Lionel made lousy water towers," says Sefton.

In one corner near the freight yard are four 444 roundhouse sections, the most valuable accessory Lionel ever made. Sefton began collecting in 1955, and accessories were one of the first things he went after. He was able to acquire good ones at low prices in the days when accessories were largely ignored by collectors.

The layout includes three power stations, five Hell Gate bridges and three terrace stations.

Sefton began working on the layout shortly after he, his wife, son, and daughter moved into the house in 1960. It was the first room that was air-conditioned.

The train room, enlarged from its original dimensions, is now 60 feet long, and the layout is spread over three garage doors covered with brown beaver board. Sefton expanded the area of the room by taking out a wall on each side and making use of former crawl spaces. The walls slope away from the center of the room, making it wider on the bottom than it is on the top.

(continued on page 128)

From the rafters to the floor, the layout room is packed with rare and valuable pieces. "The shelves have been growing down off the ceiling like stalactites," says Sefton. Lucite rods protect against earthquakes.

Tom Sefton has 219 feet of track on the mainline, 109 feet on a branch line and 263 feet in two yards — a passenger yard on one side of the room and a freight yard on the other. Sometimes in the spring ivy sprouts through cracks in the eaves, and settles on the track. "We have some neat wrecks," says Sefton. Once, a green 408E pulling five state cars derailed and fell onto the floor.

Wish fullfillment: two Lionel 128 terrace stations face one another. Why? "I always wanted two terraces on my layout," says Sefton.

"For trains you don't need all the space for head room," he says. "But there's a trade-off along the eaves. The lower you go, the more surface you can have for the trains. If you go too low, however, you make it too hard to work with." The surface is 36 inches off the floor.

Sefton has a large collection, not only of Lionel, but of American Flyer and Ives, and he collects other toys as well. He has the finest Buddy "L" collection in the country, including more than 100 freight cars, and every non-train toy Buddy "L" made. Sefton has more Buddy "L" than Buddy L had.

"Buddy never collected it," said Sefton about A. B. Lundahl, called Buddy, the man whose father owned the company until it went out of business in 1932. In 1983, Mrs. A. B. Lundahl, Buddy's widow, gave Sefton a toy plane that Lundahl owned when he was a boy. A note attached to the plane and signed by Mrs. Lundahl says, "Buddy L himself owned and played with this toy."

Sefton's train room is jammed, in almost every available cranny, with valuable trains. New crannies have been created through the years by attaching shelves to the beams in the eaves above the layout. He uses

different sections of space between rafters to show different exhibits. There is one, for instance, that shows every type of track Lionel ever made.

On shelves beneath the layout are boxed Erector sets and other boxed displays. At the end of a display in the middle of the room is the Lionel stove. Next to it are glass cases displaying items in groups: Erector set motors in one, with Lionel boats below, and boxed Lionel accessories in another. In one corner is a display of nickel-plated standard gauge steamers, and in the rafters are Lionel standard gauge paint samples. Nearby are

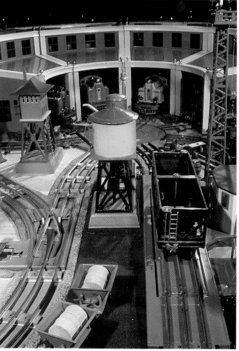

two Hiawatha sets, scale freight cars, the M-10000, a 238E with 600-series passenger cars, and four Bild-a-Locos, including an orange Macy's set.

"I can hardly resist bright, clean pieces, and orange is a particular favorite. I love orange because as a kid I would go to San Francisco with the family and see the old Key System. The ferries and the interurbans were orange. I'm sure that's why it turns me on today."

Sefton also collects European trains. He particularly likes crocodiles. In a hallway leading to the train room, behind glass, are two

ABOVE Sefton had an artist paint a city skyline in this corner. What to do with walls has always been a problem for the layout designer. LEFT A front view of the four roundhouse sections, with an Ives water tower in the foreground.

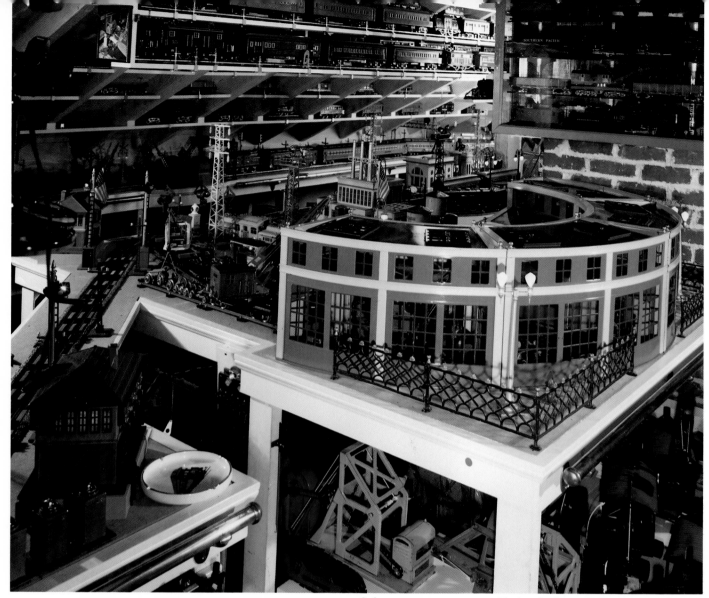

Sefton spent two years considering the layout before he started building it. He has four electric circuits and can run two trains at once. The room is weather-proofed and air-conditioned, but does not use return air, so it is always fresh. Once a year professionals come to vacuum the dust. OPPOSITE A closeup of the station.

Marklin 1 gauge crocodiles and a complete set of rare Marklin 1 gauge 57 cm. passenger cars.

Tom Sefton, 69, was born in 1917, and when he was two months old was adopted by Joseph Sefton Jr. and his wife, Helen. He knows little about his natural parents except that he came from a large Scotch-Irish family.

"I'd probably have ended up as a policeman," he says. Instead he serves on the police commission and is the third generation of his family to head the San Diego Trust & Savings Bank, the largest and oldest locally owned commercial

bank in the city. His grandfather founded the bank in 1889, his father became president in 1937 and Sefton in 1960. His son is next in line. Sefton attended Columbia University and was a combat pilot in Italy in World War II. He began collecting in 1955. He was introduced to a group of knowledgeable East Coast collectors, including Dr. Gerald Robinson and Louis Hertz, the author, as well as Irving Schull, who was selling items from the soon-to-be disbanded Lionel museum.

"Irving Schull was a nice fellow," says Sefton. "He told me to just look through pictures I had taken

of the museum collection and tell him what I wanted. Price? He said, 'Just send me what you think they're worth.' Nice. I wrote a note to his widow when he died and she wrote back."

When Sefton was ready to build a layout he knew he would not have the space for scenery, since standard gauge takes up so much room with just the trains and accessories, but he wanted things to run well. He found ⅜-inch beaver board in which B-24 engines were packed during the Second World War. He used this for the surface and then obtained more than 500 feet of extremely hard to find rubber road bed that Lionel made for its standard gauge track. The track rests loosely on the rubber bedding, allowing for a nice click of the rails as trains pass over. At the same time the rubber and beaver board keep the noise level down.

The quiet ride is necessary because Sefton likes to run his trains, as rare and as valuable as they are. The longest straightaway on the layout extends about 55 feet across a Hell Gate Bridge and down past the freight yards.

"The trains can really move on the straightaway," says Sefton. "The 408 and the other double-motored engines are the best pullers. I don't put the 400Es on the layout because the pony wheels bounce off."

Graham Claytor, now head of Amtrak, stayed with the Seftons one weekend. At that time Claytor, an avid toy train enthusiast, was President Jimmy Carter's Secretary of the Navy. The guest room is just down a train-lined hallway from the train room. At 8 o'clock Sunday morning Sefton heard noises and went to the train room. There was the head of the navy, in his pajamas, running the state cars at high speed around the layout.

"He was really *racing* them around," says Sefton. "I joined him."

On one wall of the train room is a framed cover of a 1930 Lionel catalog. It features the green 381 electric and a background of light brown, an earth-tone tan. The catalog is one that young Tom Sefton used to study under the covers at boarding school. He selected the same shade of brown as the predominant color for his layout, the color of the beaver board.

"I always looked at the catalogs and dreamed," says Sefton. "I still do. I've got the catalogs downstairs."

The man remains the boy, only he is having more fun.

Frank Sinatra
Rancho Mirage, California

Form and Function — Nice and Easy

Inside a walled entrance along the Tamarisk Country Club in Rancho Mirage, California, is the family compound of Frank Sinatra, the singer. Obviously a man of many talents, Frank Sinatra is also a man of multiple interests, and two of the buildings in the compound reflect a particular interest of his. One of the structures is a caboose, the other a train station. The caboose — actually a large flatcar rebuilt to resemble an oversized caboose — sits on trucks and a section of track and contains, among other things, a barber shop and an exercise room. The train station is a full-size reproduction of a Fundimensions model — the 2787 Arlee — and contains Sinatra's train collection and layout.

Although Sinatra had a casual interest in toy trains for a long time — even visiting the Lionel showroom in New York City back in the 1940s when he was the idol of the bobby soxers — his more serious involvement didn't begin until the 1970s, when a friend gave him a Fundimensions HO set to take along on a mountain vacation. His interest renewed, he started to accumulate some items, both rare and common.

While returning from a singing engagement in Atlantic City in 1980, he saw a picture of the Arlee station. Back home he showed it to his contractor, who then built a real life version to house Sinatra's collection. It sits on a landscaped expanse of lawn next to the caboose, an old baggage cart between them, with a wooden

rocker and a couple of captain's chairs out on the stoop beneath the eaves.

When, in early 1982, Sinatra decided to have an O gauge train layout built, he selected a design submitted by Paul Kirby of San Dimas, California, owner of the Train Stop hobby store there and an experienced layout builder.

"I went out and met with Frank," said Kirby. "I had an artist's rendering of something I thought he would be interested in. It was based on a photograph of the original Lionel layout in their display room. I also brought along the book the photo appeared in (TM's Vol. II: Postwar) and a film clip. He was just ecstatic with the idea. I said, 'That layout is huge. We're going to have to condense it. We don't know what we're going to lose.'"

The room where the layout would be was 18x30 and there would have to be a 3-foot clearance all around, leaving a layout that would measure 12x24.

"We talked for about two hours," said Kirby. "He told me some of the things he wanted and some of the things he didn't care about. But he was really interested in trying to produce this layout as close as we could to the Lionel one, understanding that we were going to have to condense and lose some things."

The photograph of the Lionel layout showed a 115 Stop Station

in the foreground, a higher elevation with some structures behind it, and mountains in the far background.

"He really liked that end shot with the 115 station. That caught his eye. He wanted an oak framework and display cases for his trains under the layout. He already had display cases on the walls. He wanted a lot of glass for the cases. He thought he saw a river and really wanted one.

"The theme of the layout was to be the '20s and '30s. He wanted something to do with New Orleans. I found out later that, of all places he ever performed, his most memorable occasions were in New Orleans."

Kirby brought up an idea of having something on the layout be reminiscent of Hoboken, New Jersey, where Sinatra was born and spent his boyhood. "He was overjoyed," said Kirby, and they decided on some brownstones.

Beginning in April of 1982 Kirby and a team of six to ten people worked 8 hours a day, 7 days a week, for 11 weeks. The first thing done, even before inside construction began, was to have the display cases built. Six 12-foot cabinets were sub-contracted to a cabinet-maker in San Bernardino. They had champagne interiors, were illuminated, had glass shelves and roller-bearing glass doors. The table top height of the layout is 44 inches, a height selected as most comfortable for Sinatra, and there

133

The building that houses Frank Sinatra's layout is a full-size version of the Fundimensions Arlee Station. It sits in a family compound of buildings, including a caboose-style car containing an exercise room. Pets abound. That's Nero chewing on a stick.

The Sinatra layout was modeled after the one in the Lionel showroom from 1949 through 1957 (see page 78). Although reduced in size, it is an accurate reproduction of the original. It features a subway level like Lionel's and the 115 city station with four 156 station platform sections. The original had ten.

is a 6-inch high railing which borders the layout and was built atop the display cabinets. So, technically, the fronts of the cabinets are 50 inches high. In April they were delivered to the train room.

"We started with the display cases," said Kirby. "We set those around the floor. Then we came in with 1x4s and built a complete grid work. That was capped off with ½-inch plywood and ½-inch Celotex. Next we built this raised area in the center, so we laid the track work down on that and built the mountain. The raised area is also covered with ½-inch plywood and ½-inch Celotex. The mountain, which rises to almost eight feet off the floor, was formed with screen

(continued on page 138)

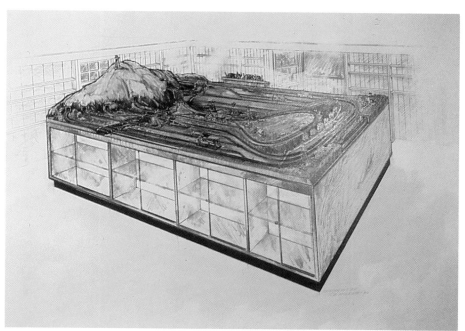

An artist's rendering of the 12x24-foot layout, showing the built-in display cabinets. The lighted oak cabinets are visible through the windows of the station on the opposite page.

Like the original in New York, Sinatra's layout has a function that does not follow its form. Five track loops run independently of each other, for dependability of operation, although Paul Kirby designed the track to look as if the loops are interconnected. Lionel had done a similar camouflage job, using lots of sidings, in their showroom. They were most concerned that the equipment would run without problems, and so was Kirby. "I knew we had to keep it in a very simple form. If we had built a complicated layout, Sinatra would have trouble and so would I. I would have lived out there making repairs."

Sinatra's collection is a mixture of what strikes his fancy, led by postwar Lionel and MPC. He has many specialty items given to him by friends. RIGHT A needlepoint freight set for his daughter, Nancy. BELOW A European engine and tender commemorating a role that allowed vocation and avocation to intermingle.

wire and Hydrocal, the traditional way — and then painted."

The surface of the Celotex was painted with ground covering, using white glue and Woodland Scenics. For track Kirby used 3-rail tinplate, with 072 wide radius curves. The track as laid down is a hybrid — some original Lionel O gauge and some of the 3-foot sections that are currently being produced.

"I originally approached the idea of using either Lionel tinplate track or Gargraves," said Kirby. "My first thought was to use Gargraves. Frank took a look at it and didn't want it. He wanted the nostalgia of the old track. So we ended up using the 072. I went to a guy in Las Vegas who has a small foundry and is reproducing the 072 switches. So the entire layout is tinplate, including the 16 switches."

Although the layout used 350 pounds of ballast material, it was only cosmetic. There is no roadbed. The track is screwed down to the Celotex. As might be expected when doing a job for someone with an ear like Frank Sinatra's, sound was a major concern to Kirby.

"I was worried we were going to have a sound problem and with a job of that magnitude you do everything you can to avoid it. In the end, it was all right. The sound was tolerable. Number one, all the noise is confined; by doing the display cases all around you didn't get a drum effect. And the carpet is super thick, which helped absorb more. Finally, the noise is deadened by the Celotex. It is very tolerable. You can talk in the room with five trains running."

There are five independent loops on the three levels of the layout. It is powered by four ZW transformers, plus supplementary power. Five trains can be run simultaneously.

Shortly before the project was completed, Sinatra said it exceeded his expectations. Kirby was pleased because Sinatra hadn't commented for a while. "I found out he is upfront about things. If he doesn't like something, you know about it the day before it happens. The absence of conversation is acceptance."

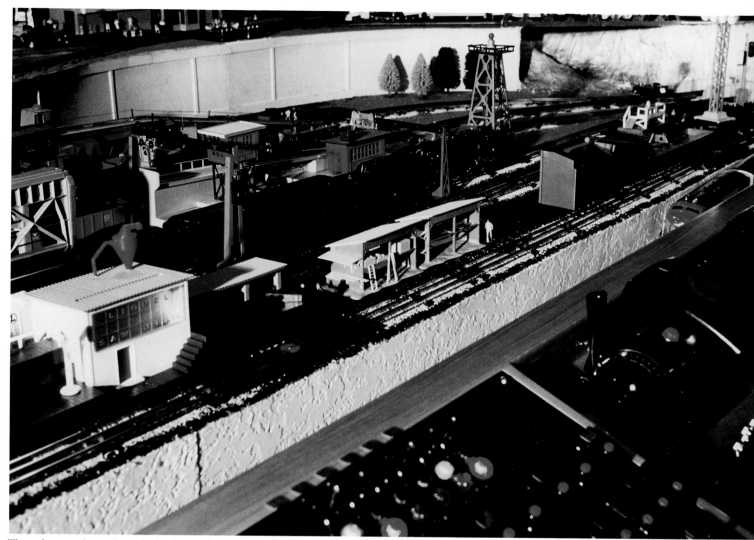

The oak control panel overlooks the straightaway in the same position as it did on its prototype in the Lionel New York showroom. Sinatra wanted plenty of postwar accessories, and got them. Every Lionel accessory but the 313 Bascule bridge, an erratic performer, is represented. The accessories are wired on separate circuits.

"The original Lionel layout looked complicated but it wasn't. I wanted to accomplish the same thing with this layout," said Kirby. "So I set everything up on a separate identity. Then he could turn this one on and run this one, and this one on and run this one, and so forth.

"Each loop has its own sidings. The one on top is just like the one Lionel built. So you can turn it loose and it just constantly runs and dogbones itself."

The layout is loaded with postwar Lionel accessories — the 97 Coal elevator, the 164 log loader, a whole series of 455 oil derricks, the

culvert loader and unloader, the operating milk car, the gantry crane and the 115 stop station.

"Frank really wanted a river, but we ran out of space," said Kirby. "If we had had another ten feet, we would have done it. Once we decided no water, we didn't have to use the bascule bridge. That made me feel more comfortable because the reliability of the bascule bridge is low."

Kirby's main goal in building the layout was to keep it operationally simple. Building a layout for someone else is quite different from

building one for yourself. The self-builder can load it with as many intricacies as he wants and know just what to do when something goes wrong. That, of course, does not apply when building for another person.

"I felt from talking to him and talking to his people, trying to get a feel for him, that we had to keep it in a very simple form," said Kirby. "He wanted to walk in and turn it on and watch the trains go around. I tried to stay with things based on my 20 years experience that would be virtually trouble free for him.

"We had to create the illusion that there was really more going on than there was. To look at the layout you would not know they were independent loops. In all my layouts I create illusions. The illusion with Sinatra was that it looked like it was all one loop.

"But anybody could walk up and operate it. All the controls are preset and labled. You want to run the gantry crane, there are labels for the gantry crane. It is all there. Independent loops."

The voltage was also made as mistake-proof as possible. Separate circuits were used for the track, accessories and switches. Kirby used MPC switch motors for the 072 switches that were made in Las Vegas.

"We bought the new switch motors from Lionel and bolted them onto the switch. I put all the switches on a separate circuit fixed at 8 or 9 volts and installed a 12 or 14-volt bulb so heat was no problem. I put the accessories on separate circuits, too, and set the voltage between 12 and 16 volts depending on which accessories were hooked into the circuit. I used the inside dials on the ZW transformers for these circuits so there would be less chance they would be moved by mistake. All you have to do is turn the master switch on and operate the trains with the big handles of the ZW."

To get such simplicity of operation took a monumental and time-consuming wiring job. Kirby used 1,800 feet of wire.

On top, the layout is not burdened by buildings or other structures. This was intentional. "We did not want to cloud the issue with structures. We wanted it to be a running layout with scenery. Something easy to maintain."

ABOVE Nine of these hand-painted porcelein cookie jars, representing Hoboken brownstones, were placed behind the train station in lieu of the hilly area that appeared on the Lionel original. BELOW Paul Kirby holds one of the unpainted jars in his San Dimas hobby store. OPPOSITE The layout is sprinkled with memorabilia of Frank Sinatra's life and career. The steamboat is representative of New Orleans, a favorite performing spot.

For the New Orleans scene, Kirby scratch built a Mississippi paddleboat, which he named the Robert E. Lee. Since there was no water, he placed the boat in dry dock and turned it into a performing center where Frank Sinatra was appearing. There is a bandstand on the boat and band members and a parking lot. There is a billboard with Sinatra's picture that announces his appearance at the Robert E. Lee. Of the 400 people on the layout, perhaps 30 or 40 are in the area of the bandstand.

To recreate the Hoboken brownstones, Kirby selected ceramic cookie jars that were shaped like buildings. He painted them in different colors and, presto, old New Jersey. They were placed in an arc at the end of the layout near the 115 station.

140

"Near the mountain there is a farm. On the bottom across the front are the brownstones," said Kirby. "In each of the corners in the front I used an MPC grain elevator, and then I used the blinking tower in the other corners."

One of the most striking features of the layout is the lighting.

"That was tremendous. There was a contractor there on staff; just the mere mention of anything I wanted and it was taken care of. I forget how many floods and spotlights were put up in the cathedral ceiling, but they are on a panel with rheostats. You can dial this thing and create morning light, evening light, high noon, shadows. And there are a tremendous number of lights on the layout itself. The effect with all the layout lights on and the rheostat set on evening light is very dramatic."

The problem of accessibility to the inner reaches of the layout, in case of derailments or other needed adjustments, was solved in rather direct manner by Kirby.

"I designed it so you can walk on it," he said. This did present a rather unusual corollary problem.

"One day I got a call from one of his aides. Frank was apparently up there walking around. The aide was very concerned. He asked me, 'Is this thing going to collapse?' Well, we had all been walking on it when we were building it. I told the guy, 'No, if it holds eight 200-pounders, I think Frank can walk around on it.'"

Sinatra's collection contains many trains that arrive as gifts from friends and therefore covers a variety of eras. He is partial to passenger service and his collection is heavy in that area.

"He likes to run long passenger trains," said Kirby. "He usually runs the long ones with double engines. There is no set thing. If he wants to run this one today, he pulls it out."

Because Sinatra enjoys passenger trains so much, one year Kirby, using part MPC equipment and part Williams, designed and built a special model of a Southern Pacific passenger train that once ran between Los Angeles and New Orleans. He dropped it off at Sinatra's on Christmas Eve. He later learned that Sinatra was up until 2 or 3 in the morning with it.

"He *does* enjoy his trains," said Kirby.

Glossary

BENCHWORK The support structure for the surface of a layout. Sometimes called gridwork.

CURVES, 072 The diameter of a 72-inch circle of track.

FUNDIMENSIONS In 1973, General Mills changed the name of its division that included Lionel trains from Model Products Corporation to Fundimensions.

GARGRAVES TRACK Track that is more realistic-looking than track made by the toy train manufacturers. Gargraves track is manufactured by the Gargraves Trackage Corporation of Rochester, New York.

GAUGE The distance between the outside rails of track. The width of O gauge track is 1¼-inches, of S gauge is ⅞-inch, of standard gauge is 2¼-inches, and of HO gauge — half O — is ⅝-inch.

HI-RAIL LAYOUT A layout where everything is scale except the trains and track.

INDEPENDENT LOOPS Loops of track with no switches.

MPC Refers to Model Products Corporation, the name given in 1970 to the division of General Mills that made Lionel trains. Even though MPC was used for only three years, through 1972, most collectors use it to refer to all Lionel trains produced after 1970.

PLASTICVILLE The brand name of structures and landscaping items that were commonly used on toy train layouts in the 1950s.

SCALE MODELERS Those operators who make layouts using trains, track, and structures that are all in exact scale.

SCALE The size relationship between the model and its real life prototype, usually expressed in a fraction. Lionel O gauge trains are approximately 1/48 the size of the real trains they are modeled after.

SCRATCH BUILT Something built by model makers — a structure or locomotive, for example — from raw materials, as opposed to something made from a kit or purchased whole.

TINPLATE Toy trains that are not in scale, as opposed to those that are. The term grew out of the fact that early toy trains were made of iron coated metals. The early track was also tin-plated. the term continues in use, even though plastic has long replaced tin as the material generally used in toy train manufacture.

TINPLATE LAYOUT A layout that uses toy trains and accessories without regard to scale size.

TINPLATERS Toy Train collectors and operators.

TOY TRAINS Mass-produced engines and rolling stock like made by manufacturers such as Lionel, American Flyer, and Marx.

TOY TRAIN LAYOUT An attempt to duplicate the real world in miniature, using simulated structures, people, trees, greenery, mountains, rivers, vehicles, and trains. Layouts can be made with strict adherence to scale (scale model layouts), without strict adherence to scale (toy train or tin-plate layouts), or with a combination of scale and non-scale (Hi-rail).